BE FREAKING AWESOME

Developing a success mindset

for a remarkable life

———

ANGELA BELFORD

Be Freaking Awesome by Angela Belford
Published by CBC Global
68 W. Sunbridge, Fayetteville, AR 72703

www.AngelaBelford.com

Book Design, Layout and Cover by Lauren Schwab, Elizabeth
Kirkendall, Jaqueline Aguilar-Vega and Taisa Akey at
The Belford Group.

Cover Photo by Joe Wittkop Photography
ISBN: 978-0-9991862-9-9

For information about special discounts available for bulk
purchases, sales promotions, fund-raising and educational needs,
contact CBC Global/The Belford Group at 479-443-9945 or
sales@AngelaBelford.com.

Contents

DEDICATED TO

Barry Belford
My Cute Freshman Boy
No words can convey the impact of your love.

Sami, Josh, and Lexi
Thank you for showing me what grace is all
about and becoming some of my best friends.

Introduction

*Are you tired? Tired of busy, tired of
overwhelmed, tired of mediocre?*

*Do you wish you could have a full life?
Deep meaningful relationships? Lots of fun?
Lower stress?*

I want to share with you how you can Be Freaking Awesome.
It's not about money or possessions—quite the opposite. It's
about joy, love, freedom, and hope. Our country is in a hope
crisis. Have you lost your ability to dream big dreams? Heck,
most of us don't even dream small dreams. A remarkable life
prioritizes experience and people over the material garbage
that cause us to dream small.

A remarkable, fulfilling, and great life begins with the
right mindset. Bad things will happen, but how do you react
to them? Do you let negative thoughts run rampant in your
mind? Do you wallow in the negative? Or do you decide that
this, your end-of-the-world moment, just makes a better
story, contains a lesson for your growth, or could lead you to a
place you couldn't have gotten to otherwise?

How do you develop the right mindset—that way of thinking that leads to joy, love, freedom? I believe it begins with a
strong faith in Jesus Christ. You may be in a different place

regarding faith, but I find a message of hope and a call to Be Freaking Awesome in the life and words of Jesus. I believe in the grace and unconditional love he taught. If you come from a different faith perspective, I hope you'll stay with me, as I believe these principles can be applied to all faiths.

After an authentic faith, living a remarkable life requires a decision. Nothing happens without a decision. You have to decide that you want to ditch that mediocre mindset that culture instills. You have to decide that what everyone else thinks about you doesn't matter. You have to decide that you and your life trajectory are more important than the dishes, the laundry, and social media.

Once you've made a decision to look at your life, you have to create a vision of who you want to be. Look carefully at your life and see what's working and what's not working. What do you currently have that are serving you well? Which ones aren't? What character traits do you want to develop? What would an ideal, well-rounded life look like?

As you look at your current character traits and the ones you want to develop, your self-awareness muscle is going to get a workout. GI Joe said, "Knowing is half the battle." When it comes to self-awareness, I agree. You can't possibly improve your character traits if you aren't aware of them. Self-awareness should not be confused with self-centeredness. Self-awareness allows you to notice the interactions in your life and determine if you want the same results or if you would like different outcomes. Self-centeredness makes everything all about you.

How far off are you from that ideal life and what steps can you take daily to move closer to that vision of an ideal life? After looking internally at who you want to become, it's time to assess your life in each area to create a baseline of where you currently are and assign a numeric value between 1 and 10. Then imagine those areas with a ranking of 10. With this vision of who you want to be and what a level 10 looks like in each area, we'll break it down and set goals. Goals serve us best when they are a combination of stretch goals to create a destination and a series of step-by-step goals to navigate our daily life.

Next, it takes a commitment. A decision is one thing, but the commitment to stay in the process the rest of your life takes it to another level. When you decide to Be Freaking Awesome, you are saying that life and success are not a destination, they are a journey. That journey will take you the rest of your life. When we talk about becoming self-aware, removing road blocks, and designing your life, that means committing to everyday growth. It means that at the end of this book—and hear me loud and clear on this one—you will not have arrived. At the end of a year, you will not have arrived. And at the end of two years, you still will not have arrived.

This journey requires courage. Courage to dream again and not just the mediocre dreams of material value, but big, exciting dreams. Courage to be willing to ask those hard questions. Courage to be vulnerable. Courage to ditch the ordinary. Notice I didn't say fearless. Courage determines there is something more important than fear. Courage feels the fear and does it anyway.

Finally, as part of your process, I believe you need to share your story with at least one other person. Whether it's a friend, a family member, a fellow traveler, or someone going through a rough time. When we share our story, we remember where we've been and how far we've come; we learn the lessons a bit deeper when we teach and offer hope to others.

I began the journey of being my awesome self in May 1998 with a nervous breakdown. I didn't stop crying for nearly two weeks. I've been on the road to being awesome ever since. That means that I endeavor to live a self-examined, intentional life where I evaluate my actions, my relationships, and my results then ask hard questions about what my motivations were, what wounds do I still have, what negative beliefs do I have, and what good fruit is there to be thankful for. It means I try to celebrate the wins and not be too hard on myself about the losses, despite wanting to be better today than I was yesterday. I'm learning to live with contentment for what I have and am today, while still hoping that tomorrow I will be stronger, healthier, and more fun.

Are you ready? Are you willing to go with me on a journey, creating a road map for you to live a remarkable life? I believe you have what it takes. I believe you can Be Freaking Awesome.

If something is important enough, even if the odds are against you, you should still do it.
- Elon Musk

A Little about Me...

Before I turned eighteen, I lived with four different families. I was adopted just after birth, experienced the death of my adopted mother, survived divorce in my new family, and endured numerous instances of sexual abuse. I lost count of the number of evictions I lived through, and we "camped" in a station wagon for six weeks. Most people expected me to end up on drugs and be a mess for the rest of my life.

Instead, I went to college on a full scholarship, have stayed married to my college sweetheart for twenty-three years and counting, have lived in the same house for fourteen years, have three fantastic children who are all nearly adults and are some of my closest friends, and have owned a small business for over eighteen years. I've traveled from Hawaii to Toronto to India with numerous trips to Florida, Colorado, and other fun vacation spots.

Along the way, I've learned some important lessons and unlearned some terrible ones from a traumatic childhood. For instance, I learned that living with four families may not be the worst thing that happens to you. It could be more traumatic to live in the same dysfunctional family for twenty years, if it takes longer to realize the way you were raised may not be the healthiest way you can live life.

Here are the other less-than-ideal lessons from my childhood:

1 year old – If I fall, people will laugh at me.

5 years old – No one listens to me, even when I am hungry.

6 years old – When things begin to go well, something bad will happen.

7 years old – Men will sometimes be there for me, until it's inconvenient.

8 years old – My pain has a cost, and I am the only person I can count on.

9 years old – I am pretty because I have a good personality.

10 years old – I am the outsider; I'm not like others.

11 years old – Everything I have ever known isn't true; I come with a monthly government check.

12 years old – It doesn't matter what I want; just make others feel better.

13 years old – My body is for men to touch.

14 years old – No matter how hard I try, it's not enough.

15 years old – My body is not my own.

16 years old – I am substandard because I am poor.

17 years old – Alcohol numbs the pain.

18 years old – Mindless sex and alcohol only numbs the pain some of the time.

As an adult, I've learned:

The journey from head to heart can be the longest road you travel.

The sins of men are visited on the generations.

Truth will set me free.

Truth is absolute.

Lies that we believed as children can affect our judgment for decades.

Healing can be instant, but we have to accept it.

Sometimes after healing we still need physical therapy to relearn how to walk.

Fear can be fatal to a dream. Obedience really is bliss.

You can't teach what you haven't learned: self-esteem is caught not taught.

I always thought that I would write this book when I had "arrived," when I had figured out all my stuff, was financially wealthy, and lived an ideal life. I realize now that I will have "arrived" when I walk into the gates of heaven, and until then it's a journey. I hope this book brings freedom from the lie that you will ever have your crap 100 percent together. I want you to live with grace and peace, knowing life is a journey.

When I read a book or attend a conference, I count it successful if I learn one new thing that changes how I think. To be different, you have to change how you think. Since I didn't have someone willing to re-parent me for another eighteen years, I had to learn which things I experienced would create strong and healthy habits and which things wouldn't. So I read. A lot. Often two or three books at the same time.

I believe we can change the trajectory of our lives with small, incremental improvements. For example, imagine a train that leaves Los Angeles heading east. Along the way if the train makes small one-percent shifts, it can arrive in New York instead of Atlanta. Occasionally in life we come to a crossroads, and we can make a ninety-degree turn or even a complete U-turn. However, I believe a more effective way of traveling through life involves a continual learning curve of one-percent improvements. More manageable and sustainable for the vast majority of humans, continuous improvement contributes to a full life.

I recently rediscovered the name of this philosophy: the kaizen method. Kaizen in Japanese means continuous improvement. Originally developed to make business more efficient, it is a powerful force when applied to our lives. Rather than trying to make a giant leap forward, focus on how today can be one percent better than yesterday.

My childhood with all its trauma and sadness could have led to a dysfunctional adulthood. Instead, I've changed my mindset and lived a life of constant improvement, and today, I can say I am freaking awesome. I want to help you get on that path to an awesome life too!

Make a Decision

The two important things I did learn were that you are as powerful and strong as you allow yourself to be, and that the most difficult part of any endeavor is taking the first step, making the first decision. - Robyn Davidson

When you ask most people how they are doing, typically you'll get one or two responses: 1. "I'm good—really busy, but good." Or 2. "I'm tired." I don't think any of us dreamed of growing up and answering the question "How are you?" with "I'm tired."

Why is it that we, as a society, are so tired? Is it because we live the lives that someone else designed for us, resulting in us busying ourselves trying to be "enough"? Are we trying to live up to expectations that tell us we aren't "right"? We don't have the "right" clothes, the "right" job, enough money, the right whatever? You've heard the expression, "We spend money we don't have to buy things we don't need to impress people we don't like." Ask college students what their major is and why they are studying it, and often they will say, "That's what my parents thought I should study."

So how do we get off this hamster wheel? How do we create the remarkable life we've always dreamed of living? It starts with a decision. We have to decide to look at our life critically in all areas and begin to define what healthy, successful, and remarkable look like to us individually.

I suspect that people don't wake up one morning and say, "I think I want a crappy marriage, with rotten kids who don't know they are loved, and I want to battle insecurity in every area of my life." Often people float along in life, never making a commitment to live intentionally, and end up in a situation riddled with insecurity and perhaps, an unsatisfying marriage. Or maybe they live a life that is fine. There's nothing really wrong, but there's also nothing intentional or exciting about their life. If you ask them what's wrong, they can't really say, just an overall feeling of discontent.

However, you may not be in either of these categories. Maybe your life is going along quite well. The kids are good, the marriage is good, and overall you are happy. Or you are single and satisfied with the progression of your life. If asked to rank your life on a scale of 1–10 in terms of how fulfilled are you, you may rank it as a 7, 8, or 9. If so, bravo! Our planet needs more people like you, and I hope this book will help you take your life to a level 10.

Most days now I would rank my life as a level 7-10. However, it didn't start that way.

My birth mother, Sheila, was eighteen and had a two-year-old son when I was born. Her sister, Kay, was three years older, married, and unable to have children, so she adopted me. A year later, Sheila had another son, and both of those sons died in a trailer fire when they were three years and three months old. Around age five is my earliest memory of being hungry. When I was six, Kay was diagnosed with cancer. My adopted dad left about three months before Kay died, and she was buried on my eighth birthday.

I went to live with my Uncle Jim in Ohio. His wife, Mary, had recently become a Christian and went to a Southern Baptist Church. So I learned a lot about the Bible and Jesus, but not a lot about grace. During this time, I learned that Sheila was my biological mother and began a long-distance relationship with her.

At age thirteen, I moved to Arkansas with Sheila, my step-dad, and two half-brothers. This was great for the first few months, until we were evicted from that house, my mom started working nights, and my step-dad began touching me inappropriately. The next summer my mom and step-dad were looking for a job, again. We spent a couple of weeks in Oklahoma City "camping" in our station wagon. Oh right, some people call that being homeless. That was the first time I spent the night in a Salvation Army homeless shelter. It's hard to imagine going from Ohio where I had lived in the same house for five years, never went without food, and certainly always had clothing.

Now we were living in a station wagon and looking for a job. I had the option to go back to Ohio, but physical comfort is nothing compared to a need to belong. With my mom and step-dad, I was their daughter. I was accepted and chosen. Identity really is the key to it all.

We moved to Northwest Arkansas, and for the first few weeks we camped in our station wagon, except when it rained. Then we stayed in the Fayetteville Salvation Army. As a fourteen-year-old girl, this was more unnerving because the women slept on one side, and the men slept on another side. The tiniest bit of security we had with my brothers and step-dad wasn't there at night. Eventually we found a house in West Fork, Arkansas, where we didn't have running water for several weeks, often didn't have food, and ended up evicted a few more times. After moving to Quitman, Arkansas, my parents got a divorce, and I went to live with my grandma to avoid living with my mom and her new, drug-dealer boyfriend. I got good grades, was a cheerleader, and always loved school because it was an escape.

I think one of the reasons I abhor bad teachers is because I know for some children school is their only escape from a crappy life.

Blessed with natural intelligence and academic abilities, I received a full scholarship to the University of Arkansas. During my freshman year, I made my first conscious decision to choose a remarkable life. I decided that I wouldn't date anyone seriously until I liked myself and liked who I was. I proceeded to date a lot of people not seriously, and I had a lot of fun.

Seeing that I needed some outside counsel, one of my friends signed me up for an appointment with the counseling center on campus. I spent three to four months working on my issues, the worst of which was denial. I began to see how I used alcohol and sex to numb the ever-louder voices in my head that said I wasn't worth much. After that semester, the therapist I was seeing left the center, so I stopped going.

In January of my sophomore year, I was at lunch with my friends and I randomly announced, "I like me, I like what I'm about, and I would be my friend." They looked at me strangely since they'd all decided a year before that they liked me and would be my friend. For me, it proved an important acknowledgment.

That's the night a cute freshman boy, as my friends and I called Barry Belford, agreed to accompany me to review a band for an international reggae festival I was planning. Great cover to get a date, right? We pretty quickly began dating seriously and exclusively. By December, he bought the ring and I said yes. Then we failed the home pregnancy test, and I thought I had ruined my life. Barry and I got married, and I took one semester off to have the baby. Then three semesters later, just before our daughter Sami's second birthday, I finished my bachelor's in marketing management. Around this time, I joined Mary Kay Cosmetics as a beauty consultant.

To quiet the nagging voices in my head, I set out to prove I was worthwhile and valuable. I began qualification for a company-provided car, a Pontiac Grand Am, the first car awarded to consultants. During this qualification period, I went back to the counseling center on campus to try to get help with the issues that were holding me back, but I didn't connect with the counselor at all. He only gave me one good piece of advice, "You need a mom mentor." My sweet friend, Paula, agreed to mentor me and probably didn't know it was a lifetime commitment.

I completed qualification for the car within twelve months of joining the company. At that time in our area, most people spent three to four years earning their car. Despite qualifying in record time and being the youngest car driver in my area, I still wasn't satisfied, especially at night when I was alone with my thoughts.

So, I set my sights on the next level of achievement, becoming a sales director. I also decided I wasn't good at children's games, so we began trying to have another child, found a house to buy, and figured out that if Barry took summer classes and full-time classes, he could finish his degree before Sami's fourth birthday.

In 1997, I delivered Josh on September 5 and then finished my directorship qualification September 30, while Barry worked forty hours a week and took fifteen hours of college classes.

In May, as Barry finished his computer information systems degree, his mom came into town from Canada for a few weeks for his graduation. I had spent nine months striving to maintain the requirements to be a Mary Kay Sales Director, otherwise known as trying to "be valuable." Not only that, but this job required a commanding public presence and the appearance that you had it all together. But I didn't have it all together, and it all came crashing down. I broke. I started crying, and I couldn't seem to stop. I had reached a point where I cried every day and often couldn't make myself get out of bed, even to take care of our three-year-old daughter and nine-month-old son. One day Barry asked, "I don't get it. Why now? It's over, I've got a job, I'm done with school. Why are you breaking down now?" I wasn't articulate enough to say, "Because I can. I don't have to carry the load anymore."

During this week-long cry-fest, my senior director, who had become like a mom to me, invited me to lunch. She asked me, "Honey, what can I do to help you?" Seemed like a reasonable question to ask someone who had been crying for a week.

I said, "I think I need help." She replied, "What do you want to do?" I told her I wanted to check myself into a treatment facility. We went in her pink Cadillac to the resident psychiatric facility. She said, "Well, sweetie, you sure know how to go in style." We walked into the facility where I thought I'd start crying again, when they said, "I'm sorry, ma'am, without insurance there's nothing we can do."

Luckily, my senior director and the pastor of my church lived in the same neighborhood. She called him, and he got me an appointment the next day with a wonderful counselor, Joe Young. Over the next thirteen months, he proved to be the Mighty Joe Young, though luckily not a gorilla like the famous Disney movie. They say third time's a charm, and I could only hope my third time to therapy at age twenty-four would be different. There had to be a better way. I knew I could learn a better system.

After a couple of sessions of therapy, God and I had a little chat. I had visited Terra Studios where they made these beautiful glass sculptures, the Blue Birds of Happiness. To make the  glass, the glass blower had to get the glass really, really hot, and then they rolled the glass, using shears to trim the unnecessary pieces. I said to God, "Listen, I will do the work, I will engage, I will do my part. But you have to do your part. I want you to make this as hot, as hard and as fast as possible. In the end, I want you to form me into a beautiful glass pitcher that you use to pour out your love on other people. If I am not going to go through this pain for myself. To get healthy for just me isn't worth it. You must use me to help others get healthy."

God answered that prayer. Those thirteen months were some of the hardest I had ever experienced because I had to relive the first twenty-four years of pain. I had to learn that when you decide to never hurt again, you also limit your ability to feel love and joy. As if seeing my life for the first time, I recognized that I had created the life I was experiencing. I had allowed the things that happened to me to shape what I thought of myself. For me, it began with a decision. I decided to look critically at my life and figure out why I didn't like who I was when I went to bed at night. I wanted to quiet those voices in my head.

It All Begins with a Decision

The first decision is to look at your life critically to see what works and what does not work. In the next chapter, we'll begin designing your life, but first we have to be very clear on why we are making a decision.

Over the years, I've met people who aren't sure they need to look at their life critically. They may be in denial and have decided their life is fine or that they currently don't have time to stop and examine their life. Some may say they don't have time because of the kids. "As a working parent, right now I have to focus on working and providing for my children. I will work on myself and get healthy after the kids leave." ARRRGGGGGH. Seriously? Then how will our kids have any idea of what a healthy, well-adjusted adult looks like? Once they move out on their own, your opportunity to show them how to live well diminishes greatly. Typically, they will do what we do, not do what we say. Plus, in your unhealthiness you are going to pass on your insecurities, and you will hurt them, whether you mean to or not. Then they not only have to get over the bad example you showed them because of your pain, but they also have their own wounds that you inflicted.

Have you ever played hide and seek with a small child who believes "if I can't see you, you can't see me?" Perhaps another reason we don't want to look critically at our life is that we believe if we don't acknowledge our flaws then others won't see them. As we like to say, "Denial is not just a river in Egypt."

A close relative of denial and another reason we don't look at our lives critically is fear. Later I've devoted a whole chapter to addressing your fears. At this point, I want to remind you of Zig Ziglar's acronym for fear – False Evidence Appearing Real

Fear can play an important role in our survival. It's our brain's way of saying, "It's time to be on high alert." Sometimes we take that message and translate it to mean, stop what you are doing. Instead, if we can listen to the fear, get curious about what's causing the fear, and calmly reassure our brain that we are listening and we are proceeding cautiously, then the fear can be useful. We can take the first step to deal with fear. Right now, let's tell our brains that the decision isn't scary; we are just going to look at our lives. You don't even have to commit to doing anything about it, just decide to look at it.

So, do you want your life to get better? Are you ready to make a decision to go on this journey? Congratulations, you've completed the first step to Be Freaking Awesome.

The secret to getting ahead is getting started.
- Mark Twain

Create a Vision

Instead of looking at the past, I put myself ahead twenty years and try to look at what I need to do now in order to get there then." - Diana Ross

After you've decided to Be Freaking Awesome, it's time to create a clear vision of how you want to travel on this journey. When you make this decision, you are saying that despite everything that has or is happening to me, you can choose the kind of person you want to be. Let's create that vision.

By the time I went to college, I had moved around so much that the longest friendship I had was three years, and the longest I'd ever lived with anyone was about five years. I didn't know a lot about long-term relationships. I can remember people saying, "Well, I have to do this thing because it's my brother." I had no point of reference for the loyalty they were talking about. I sort of fumbled my way through, experiencing conflict and resolution as I figured out the character traits that made up who I was. I lost a lot of relationships, I hurt people inadvertently, and I was blessed with some extremely kind and patient friends.

What Character Traits Do You Want?

Think about those kind friends you have. If you made a list of characteristics you think of when you consider a good friend might be the same characteristics you would like in yourself: someone who listens well, laughs a lot, loves well, spreads kindness, is gentle, doesn't take themselves too seriously, loves adventure, doesn't complain, cheers you on, cries with you when you are down, and reminds you of your awesomeness when you forget.

I believe that being a good friend will translate into every area of your life. Read the list again starting with a good wife/husband. What about good mom/dad. Read the list again starting with a good daughter/son. I would say most of those characteristics are also the things you'd want in a good boss/employee/coworker.

So, you see, in all your relationships it pays off just to be a good friend—you know, Be Freaking Awesome.

Write It Down

Below there is a list of possible character traits you might want to cultivate (ideonomy.mit.edu/essays/traits.html). Sometimes our tendency is to focus on the things we aren't doing well and not give ourselves credit for the things we do well. Read through the list the first time looking for traits that **you currently have and circle them**. Next, read back through the list for traits that **you want to develop and underline** those traits. The reason we underline them is so that as you develop them, you'll be able to change the underline to a circle. Add any character traits you are interested in developing.

Active	Balanced	Clever
Adaptable	Calm	Compassionate
Adventurous	Capable	Confident
Agreeable	Caring	Conscientious
Appreciative	Charismatic	Considerate
Articulate	Charming	Contemplative
Aspiring	Cheerful	Cooperative

Courageous	Humble	Punctual
Courteous	Humorous	Purposeful
Creative	Idealistic	Rational
Curious	Imaginative	Realistic
Daring	Independent	Relaxed
Decisive	Innovative	Reliable
Dedicated	Insightful	Resourceful
Disciplined	Intuitive	Respectful
Discreet	Joyful	Responsible
Efficient	Kind	Responsive
Empathetic	Likes Silliness	Romantic
Energetic	Logical	Sensitive
Enthusiastic	Lovable	Simple
Fair	Loyal	Skillful
Faithful	Mature	Sober
Flexible	Moderate	Spontaneous
Focused	Modest	Stable
Forgiving	Objective	Steady
Friendly	Observant	Strong
Fun-loving	Optimistic	Subtle
Generous	Organized	Sympathetic
Gentle	Original	Team Player
Genuine	Passionate	Thorough
Good Attitude	Patient	Thoughtful
Good-natured	Peaceful	Tolerant
Has grace	Perseverance	Trusting
Hardworking	Personable	Understanding
Healthy	Persuasive	Warm
Helpful	Polished	Well-read
Honest	Practical	Well-rounded
Honorable	Prudent	Wise

How do you feel? Ideally, you feel hopeful that you have direction in the area you want to travel.

One of the easiest ways for me to figure out a character trait I need to work on is to notice the people in my life who annoy me the most. I begin to get curious about what trait in them is something I do not like about myself. When I first discovered this phenomenon, I was horrified. That person is so obnoxious—oh, sometimes I can be obnoxious. That person isn't friendly to everyone—oh, sometimes I can be unfriendly. It's so incredibly humbling and even hard to appreciate the lesson, but it's also extremely enlightening.

Now that you've identified some character traits you'd like to develop, let's try a few more ideas to develop your life vision

Epitaph

When I was 26 and pregnant with my youngest daughter, Lexi, I attended Jack Canfield's ten-day Facilitating Skills Seminar in Santa Barbara, California. It's designed to teach you skills to create and lead self-esteem workshops. A lot of the training is spent working on ourselves to be ready to help others. Two exercises really helped me design my vision for a Level 10 life.

First, we had to write our epitaph. We had to think about how we wanted to be remembered by our family. Mine was:

Faithful Christian

Devoted Wife

Loving Mother

Brilliant Entrepreneur

Often in my life when I have an important decision to make, I look at it from this perspective, taking the longest view. Some people may think of this as morbid, but I think it can help us create a more long-term approach to life where the little, day-to-day things don't have as much weight. As you are creating your life vision, consider writing your epitaph, your great guide for life, and your family may thank you.

Life Purpose Statement

The second exercise that helped me was creating a life purpose statement. We did a guided visualization where we went to a mountaintop and met a sage who gave us a box with our life purpose in it. Mine was:

> *Love and Empower People.*
> *Spread the message of hope.*

Until I was thirteen, my name was Jenny, short for Geneva, the first name I shared with my grandma. When I moved to Arkansas, I changed my name to Angela. I later discovered the meaning is messenger of hope. I believe God planted this purpose in my mind as a young girl, making it completely natural to change my name.

Look carefully at your life to discover the things that may be pointing you to your life purpose. If you don't discover it, don't let it bog you down. Be open to the revelation.

Level 10 Living

Each coach I've had on my journey has had some version of this exercise. It's a wheel that asks you to rank your life on a scale of 1 to 10 in several different areas. It's designed to determine how I felt about each area of my life. The last time I did it, the coach asked me, "What would a level 10 look like in that area?" It changed the conversation for me.

Any area that was 5–9 I classified as one I "had to work on." But I had not considered what it would look like to be a level 10 in that area. After reworking the exercise from that perspective, I found many areas that I had ranked a 7, but I couldn't think of how it could be better than it was. I suspect that as I grow I will find ways to improve on the current 10, but for me it's a much better question.

Complete the Wheel of Life exercise. Rate your life in each of these areas on a scale of 1–10.

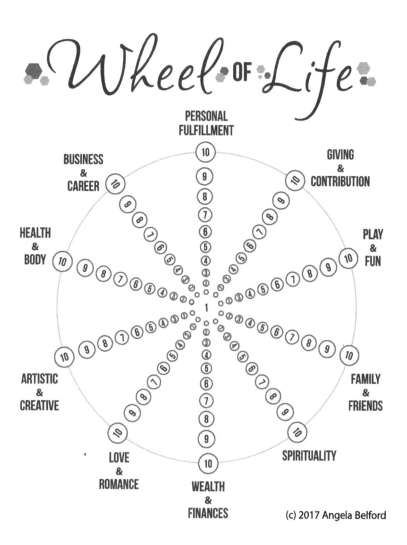

Wheel OF **Life**

PERSONAL FULFILLMENT

BUSINESS & CAREER

GIVING & CONTRIBUTION

HEALTH & BODY

PLAY & FUN

ARTISTIC & CREATIVE

FAMILY & FRIENDS

LOVE & ROMANCE

SPIRITUALITY

WEALTH & FINANCES

(c) 2017 Angela Belford

Notice if your "tire" looks out of balance in one area. It's hard to drive a car on a flat tire. Your life is the same way. If you have an area of your life that is not a 10, then look at that area as an area of growth.

Now that you've rated it, in any area of your life that's not a 10, describe what a level 10 life would look like. This is not the time to set goals; we'll get to that later. This is your time to use your imagination. Also, be somewhat realistic. If you currently make $50,000 a year, level 10 might not be making $1 million a year. I'm not exactly sure what your level 10 is, but it must be something you can vividly imagine. My caution for not overstating comes from years of setting unrealistic expectations for myself and then feeling like a constant failure.

Relax—Your Vision May Change

Sometimes people freeze at this point in the process. They are afraid that if they choose where they want to go and commit, then that is the only place they can go. As I mentioned I believe that this life is a journey. That means that if you choose a destination, after you get there you'll need to choose the next place to go. It's important to be super clear on where you want to go and what you want your life to look like. Some background on how your brain works will help you find that vision and stay focused on your journey.

Your brain has a part called the Reticular Activating System (RAS). It notices things that match what you've been thinking about and what you believe. For instance, if you buy a blue Honda, suddenly you notice all the blue Hondas on the road. Those Hondas were there last week, you just hadn't dialed in your RAS. By being clear on what you want your life to look like, you dial in your RAS so that it notices things it previously didn't. Let's say you want a life that includes a peaceful home. Then when you have dinner with your family filled with laughter and silliness and no arguments or complaining, your RAS will suddenly notice and want to accomplish more of that. Once you have had six to eight dinners in a row that have laughter and great conversation, then you have one rough night, your brain will recognize the pattern, and it will not blow things out of proportion and freak out. It will begin to believe, "I live in a home of peace and laughter" and will continue to help you create that vision.

In his outstanding book *The Power of Consistency*, Weldon Long explains that the process of programming your RAS so that your goals become as second nature to you as driving home from work, you must visualize your ideal world. That's why it's important to choose level 10 living that you can actually imagine. It involves thinking of each detail of your life and then visualizing that in positive current reality. For instance, one goal of mine is time freedom. When I visualize my ideal life, I imagine getting up, doing yoga, talking to my husband while I get ready, writing or blogging, taking care of clients at my marketing agency, lunch with a friend, dinner with family or friends, and a relaxing evening. I recently had a day that was almost this exact thing (missed yoga). I did a huge happy dance. I was able to add a lot more joy by celebrating the success of a day with time freedom.

As you begin to get clear on what level 10 living looks like, consider these questions:

What kind of fun do you like to have?

Do you want to have lots of strong relationships or do you prefer a small number of deep relationships?

Do you want to have a very active social life or do you prefer reading?

Do you want your home to be a place of peace or a place that is full of people and laughter?

Do you want your immediate family to be healthy?

Do you want to raise children who are independent and well-adjusted adults?

Considering these questions will help you clarify your vision of who you want to be, what character traits you value, and what your level 10 life will look like. Now let's examine our beliefs and thoughts.

It Begins with Beliefs

Your beliefs become your thoughts.
Your thoughts become your words.
Your words become your actions.
Your actions become your habits.
Your habits become your values.
Your values become your destiny.
- Mahatma Ghandi

My uncle Jim loved to garden. He found it relaxing to go out and plant tomato plants and take care of them all season and then harvest the yummy vegetables. My favorite was eating the cherry tomatoes. The rest of it just seemed like a lot of work. But each year he would get out the tiller, break up the ground, and create rows, and then we kids would help him plant the garden. Even though we lived right in town, he had a huge vegetable patch.

Tomatoes are my favorite vegetable. I really like to make salsa and find that the tomatoes with a lot of meat and not a lot of juice actually make the best salsa. There are many varieties of tomatoes, when I buy tomato plants at the nursery, I have to depend on the little tab that has a picture on it to trust what kind of tomato I am going to get. I have to buy the plant, take it home, plant it, water it, add Miracle Grow, keep the deer away from it, and take care of the plant for several months before the tomatoes are ready to harvest. If some-one has mislabeled the plants, I could end up with cherry tomatoes when I wanted Big Burpee tomatoes. I love cherry tomatoes, but they don't work well for salsa. Worse, what if I thought I was getting tomatoes and actually ended up with a different kind of plant entirely.

Like tomato plants, beliefs are "planted" in our subconscious mind. Then our Reticular Activating System (RAS) helps us notice the situations that will make that belief true. Your mind hates to be wrong. It will work overtime to prove you right. If you have a belief that people are out to get you, your mind will notice every time something happens to you to confirm that belief. It will actually ignore situations that disprove that belief, sort of like the blue Hondas you now notice. If you have a belief that people are good, kind, and doing the best they can, then when someone does something counter to that belief you will likely either not notice, not be offended by it, or decide it's an exception. Your brain won't remember the times that people weren't kind. If someone tries to point out unkindness and how often it has happened to you, you'll likely think it's a fluke.

My husband used to ask me near the end of an argument, "What do you want me to do?" I completely exasperated him by saying, "I want you to figure out why you did what you did." I would attempt to explain that if I just told him what to do, then when he was stressed, tired, or sick he would revert back to acting out of his beliefs. One day during an argument about our business, I said, "If you would just decide that when I find errors in your software it means I am a strong team member and I make your software better. Instead, you think when I find errors that I am saying you don't have value." The next day a typical argument started when I found an error with the software. Instead of getting defensive, he said, "I'm glad you found it instead of the client." It was so shocking that both my employee and I stared at him with gaping mouths.

Overnight, he didn't have to think about his behavior, he simply had changed his belief.

In my twenties, I would tell my story of living with four families before age eighteen as if it was a Shakespearean tragedy. Poor me. Then, as I looked around at other people who had been with the same family for twenty years, I saw that the concept, "just because it was how you were raised doesn't make it right," was particularly difficult to grasp. I came to believe that living with four families made me great at sales. I had to learn how to make new friends and quickly assess a situation to ensure that I was safe and got my needs met. No longer was living with four families a tragedy; I believe it's a gift that has let me travel through my healing journey as an adult that much faster.

Just because it was how you were raised doesn't make it right

The grooves in my brain from childhood were at most five years deep. It's much easier to get out of that rut.

If I wanted a different life than I had growing up, I had to plant a new belief system. One that served me and created the life I wanted to live. I couldn't just whack off the old beliefs. That's like taking a weed eater to a bunch of dandelions; they will grow right back.

I also had to look seriously at what kind of fruit I wanted in my life. If you plant tomato seeds, does it make any sense to get mad when you don't have cucumbers? If I wanted cucumbers, I had to plant cucumber seeds. If I wanted a remarkable life, I had to decide what one looked like. Just as you began doing in the last chapter, I had to create a vision.

To create a new vision for my life, I knew I had to learn a new way of living. I sought learning by reading. I read *Think and Grow Rich* by Napoleon Hill. I embraced the idea that what the mind can conceive and believe it can achieve.

My Beliefs

They say that your story is not what happens to you, it's what you think about what happens to you. I'll take that a step further: your life becomes what you tell yourself.

If I followed my family's legacy, I would be a fifth-generation alcoholic. In college, alcohol became my fuel of choice. Over time, I realized that having a beer because it tastes good is different than drinking to numb my pain or to take the edge off. Even today, I have to be aware of why I'm drinking. While I do not live with the identity that I am an alcoholic, sometimes I need to order a cranberry and Sprite to ensure I'm just drinking socially and not to self-medicate or relieve stress. If that drink doesn't seem like enough, I know it has to be, otherwise I risk making bad decisions. Here's what I had generally believed about my story:

Perspective: I am homeless.

Yes, I had been without a home when I was fourteen. My home had become a station wagon with my mom, dad, and two brothers. Living in a station wagon shook my foundation and left me feeling vulnerable, but now it gives me a lot of compassion and empathy for people experiencing homelessness.

I often share my home with friends who need a place to restart and give them a chance to witness healthy family life.

Perspective: I am hungry.

My earliest memory of being hungry happened at age five. I remember lying in a bed in a trailer wondering why there wasn't even peanut butter and jelly to eat. Ironically, I've discovered the hungry little girl that lives inside me is what drives me to help others escape the bondage of their negative thoughts and beliefs so they can stop being hungry for a life of freedom. As an adult, I've also found that the little girl speaks out anytime I'm not taking good care of myself.

Perspective: I am abused.

Before the sexual abuse by my step-dad started, he and I were really close. We talked all the time and debated politics. He also taught me to drive. I figured out that the abuse lasted nine months, but the unforgiveness lasted ten years. Anytime we carry unforgiveness, we carry on their abuse. Most people wait their whole lives for an apology; I had to wait another fifteen years after I forgave him before he apologized. During that time, we didn't have a close relationship, but I did have an opportunity to invite him to my home to prove I am past this place of unforgiveness.

What about you? What beliefs define you? What belief do you need to change, to dig out and replace with a new belief? What are the stories that you tell yourself? What are the stories you believe about you? Be sure to carve out time to work on you. It is the most important gift you can give to your friends and family.

Thoughts

Your beliefs don't just stay dormant in your mind; they can grow up and become thoughts. Sometimes we believe our thoughts are random occurrences, but I think they are the result of long-held beliefs. Our thoughts can get us into trouble or keep us out of trouble.

What if you spend each day thinking of all the bad things that have happened to you in your life? You review the negative, feel what it felt like, and then operate from the negative place to continue experiencing this bad stuff. Maybe you've heard someone say, "I never get the right opportunity." "It never seems to work out for me." "I'm sure my luck won't hold out." Those are some seriously negative thoughts that express some deep beliefs.

Our home is named Rest Haven. It has been the place for at least seven adults to come and begin fresh. One such person needed to get out of a bad situation and financially couldn't afford to leave the abusive relationship. She moved in with us and for the most part was a happy, joyful person and so grateful for the opportunity for a fresh start. But on a near daily basis, she said the most negative things about her life. She would say, "I'm sure I'll never find the love of my life." "I'm sure that won't work out. Nothing ever works out." It was odd because she was not negative or whiney about these situations; she was very straightforward, just accepting her lot in life. No need to be upset about it. These were just the facts, ma'am.

I routinely said, "Stop saying that. You don't know that's true. God's really big." She would roll her eyes. I would say, "Do not affirm that. It takes just as much energy to believe the truth as it takes to believe a lie." She would be super annoyed with me because I couldn't tolerate someone saying negative things around me especially at home, and she felt I just wasn't in touch with reality.

One night she was on the phone with a friend in the other room, so I could only hear her side of the conversation. She was saying, "Do not affirm that. It takes just as much energy to believe the truth as it takes to believe a lie. Stop saying that. You don't know that's true. God's really big." I started laughing in the other room. She paused her conversation long enough to yell, "Shut up, Angela." She finally got what I was trying to say.

Sometimes you may not know what the beliefs are that are causing the thoughts and words. When you decide to Be Freaking Awesome, you will need to explore those thoughts to try to find the beliefs behind them.

Ever get a new car and an indicator light comes on that you don't recognize? I bought a used Toyota Hybrid Camry, and when the weather warmed up a light came on that had a half circle with squiggly lines at the bottom and an exclamation point in the center. I had no idea what that light meant and had to check the user manual to figure out that my tire pressure was low.

As we increase our self-awareness, which we'll cover more in depth in the next chapter, we can begin to use thoughts as indicator lights instead of treating every thought as truth and letting it wreak havoc on our emotions.

In her book *Rising Strong*, Brené Brown shares a concept called "the Story I'm telling myself." The idea is that when something happens or someone says something to you, you begin a dialogue in your head. If you see someone at an event or party and they don't acknowledge you, in your mind you may begin this: "What's wrong? Why didn't they wave at me or acknowledge me? Are they mad at me? Did I do something to them? Oh yeah, well if anyone should be mad, it's me. Remember that time when they were so insensitive?" And on and on. I don't know if guys do this as much as women do, but I know it's exhausting. A few minutes later, the person walks over to you and says, "I thought that was you! But when you walked in, the sun was behind you, and I couldn't tell." We just got all upset for nothing.

When we are upset, it is helpful to slow down and think about the story we are telling ourselves. Brené Brown encourages us to tell our spouses or friends about the story we are telling ourselves so they can help us find the truth.

The stories we tell ourselves, the thoughts we think, can lead us to discover beliefs that may be holding us back. Unfortunately, we don't have a user manual like the one that comes with our cars. We have to be willing to explore those thoughts and beliefs, and it's not easy. It can be quite difficult if you are unaccustomed to living an examined life. You may have never stopped to think about the relationship between your thoughts and the type of life you continue to experience.

Try this exercise: When you have a negative thought, write it down. Do this for three days. At first, we aren't going to do a lot of exploration on that thought; we are just going to write it down. After three days, read over the list. Are there themes in the negative thoughts?

For instance, when you interact with your kids, do you think, "When are they going to remember to pick up their shoes?" What belief could be triggering this thought? You don't have to get it right the first time; just write down what comes to mind when you consider, "What belief might be causing this thought?"

When I tried this, I came up with a vague idea about responsibility. I sat with this a bit longer and considered, "Do I believe that not picking up their shoes means they aren't being responsible?" I thought about this longer and dismissed it, because I believe my kids are very responsible. Then I asked myself, "Why does it upset me when they don't pick up their shoes?" The idea of consideration floated into my mind. So, I asked myself, "Do I believe that not picking up their shoes means they aren't considerate?" Bingo! I have discovered that I have a very strong sense of consideration. I believe that being respectful of others means that you are considerate of how your actions affect others. I explored this a bit further: "Is it true that my child is being inconsiderate or is she just being a forgetful child?" In this scenario, I choose to accept that teenagers sometimes kick their shoes off and aren't being intentionally inconsiderate. They are just being forgetful kids.

In her book *Loving What Is*, Byron Katie tells a story of how she figured out that the only person in her house bothered by the dirty socks in the living room was her. She decided that rather than cause turmoil by constantly nagging her family to pick up their socks, she chose to pick them up herself and create peace. Ironically, over time the family saw her example and started picking up their socks. She had nagged for years to no avail, but just doing it lovingly as an act of service made her family more aware.

Loving What Is also introduces four questions that can help you discover the underlying belief.

(1) Is it true?

(2) Can I absolutely know it is true?

(3) How do I react when I think that thought?

(4) Who would I be without the thought?

These questions have helped me immensely over the years. It reminds me of the quote: "Would you rather be right or happy?"

When you first begin to follow your negative thoughts to find the beliefs, it may seem overwhelming if you have a lot of negative thoughts. Be gentle with yourself. You didn't get to a point of negative thinking overnight, so you won't get out of it overnight. This is a journey, it's a process, take it slow. Be considerate of yourself.

Some of you may not be able to find the negative belief. Jack Canfield teaches a concept called Cancel, Cancel. When a negative thought appears in your mind or comes out your mouth, you say, "Cancel, cancel," and rework it with a new thought.

This is similar to when I would say to Shannon, "Stop saying that. You don't know that's true. God's really big." Restate the thought in a way that is more true, more loving, more peaceful, and more beneficial to your journey.

Feelings

Have you ever been having a good day and someone makes an offhand remark that puts you in a bad mood for a couple of hours? Maybe you walk in the door from a good day at work, and your spouse immediately gets upset because you forgot to stop and buy the one ingredient needed for dinner.

One of the most overlooked keys to a successful life involves emotional regulation and resiliency. I consider the ability to process and respond to our emotions and feelings to be vital to our success. James Allen, considered one of the pioneers of the self-help movement, wrote in 1903 in *As a Man Thinketh*, "Every action and feeling is preceded by a thought."

Your thoughts can create feelings. If you don't believe me, think about receiving a letter from the IRS. If you start thinking, "Oh crap, did I make a mistake? Am I getting audited? Oh, this is going to suck." How do you feel? Scared, anxious, fearful. What if you look at the letter and think, "This could be my lucky day. I could be getting a refund." How are you going to feel? Excited, optimistic, joyful. You don't know what's in the letter yet, and still your thoughts create feelings with it.

Here's another example: Have you ever woken up and been mad at your spouse? She asks you what's wrong. At first you can't figure it out, and then you realize you had a dream where she was a complete jerk and you were mad at her. When this happens, my husband has said, "That wasn't me. That was dreamland Barry. Please don't be angry at real Barry for something the guy in the dream did." Your spouse didn't do anything; your thoughts made you angry.

Jack Canfield teaches in *Success Principles*, the formula E+R=O. Event plus our Response equals the Outcome.

Event—Someone cuts you off in traffic.

Response—You respond in anger, screaming at the person, flipping them off.

Outcome—The outcome is that you just gave your body a major hit of cortisol, a stress hormone; your blood pressure is up; and you are now angry. It might put you in a bad mood for a few hours.

OR...

Event—Someone cuts you off in traffic.

Response—You respond with, "They must not have seen

me or they must really need to get somewhere, like maybe the hospital or a big meeting. I should give them a bit more space."

Outcome—The outcome is neutral or positive. You feel good about giving someone grace, and you go back to visualizing an amazing life and thinking of how much you love your family, grateful that you didn't get in a car accident.

The car cutting you off didn't make you angry. Your thoughts made you angry. Next, let's continue to look at the concept that no one can make you feel anything.

Drawbridge

In *Why Is This Happening to Me ... Again?!* Michael Ryce describes a scene,

Imagine we place a person from the jungle beside a river and ask him to figure out what causes a drawbridge to open. He observes, time after time, that the bridge goes up when a boat arrives. He further notes that when the boat passes, the bridge lowers. Our observer, not being familiar with bridges, comes to the obvious conclusion that boats cause bridges to go up! You and I know that it's the motor on the bridge, more specifically a cable attached to the motor that makes the bridge go up. The boat is simply a trigger in the process. So, when someone says something to us, they literally can't "make us angry." Just as the boat doesn't make the drawbridge go up, their words are a trigger to create a thought that creates a feeling of being angry.

When I first read this, I was dumbfounded. I had heard that I could control my emotions, but I always said, I wouldn't get angry if he wouldn't do XYZ. Essentially Michael Ryce was saying that XYZ wasn't making me angry. What I thought about XYZ was causing the anger.

Emotionally, when a boat comes down your river, do you automatically raise the bridge and get angry or hurt or another negative emotion? If so, you are letting the boat dictate your emotional life.

I shared this drawbridge concept in a recent workshop, and a few months later I got a text from one of the participants that said, "Today I didn't raise the drawbridge when someone said something hurtful. Thank you!" That's a win, my friends.

Ryce's process encourages you to figure out why the action of another caused a negative emotion and figure out the first time it made you angry or reminded you of something else that made you angry. That is the root issue. If you can go back and diffuse that initial issue, you go a long way toward solving today's problem.

When I was a kid, I was told all the time that "if your head wasn't attached to your body, you wouldn't know where it was." All the time. Hindsight tells me that I was undiagnosed ADD. (Thom Hartmann in *Attention Deficit Disorder: A Different Perception* says only in America is it a disorder. In Zimbabwe, I would be a hunter, a revered member of the tribe. Just saying.)

During my twenties and thirties, if someone said anything related to the "head attached to body" comment, my head would cease to be attached because it would spin like the Chucky doll. Zero to psychotic in 2.2 seconds. At the time someone said it, I didn't have the words to say, "That is still a wound. Please do not make fun of me about losing stuff because while I love being harassed about practically everything, don't go there."

Today it's less of a wound and more of a scar. But just in case, recently I was with a new friend, and we'd discovered that we like to tease each other. I lost several things within a few days, so I warned her, "Hey, please don't say these words, I am not sure how I'll react." I'm also getting much better about having a place for everything. Now I get annoyed when I don't have a place to put something.

At this point, you've spent a few days writing down your negative thoughts and examining them. Sometimes people find that exercise very hard because they don't even see that a thought is negative; it's just fact for them. Maybe this will be easier: Each time you experience an emotion that you don't want to experience as a result of a circumstance or someone's behavior (anger, anxiety, fear), write it down. You may not be able to analyze the feeling while you are having the initial emotional reaction, but find time to explore the feeling and when you first remember experiencing it. I point to being picked last on the playground as the shorthand for whenever I felt left out as a child. As you begin to unpack when you first felt this feeling, allow the adult you to reassure the child in your head that this situation is different. As an adult, you have the ability to make different choices, and you don't have to protect yourself with anger or anxiety or whatever the emotion is. Instead, you can set healthy boundaries, and you can stand up for yourself with your words and actions. When you first experienced the feeling, you may have also believed things that aren't true or decided that you would "never _____ ever again." Trust, believe, love, or whatever was connected to the emotion. If this is something that doesn't make a lot of sense, keep reading. It can take time for our brain to process new ideas. I've read books and missed an entire concept that I wasn't ready to learn until I re-read the book years later.

Behavior

I was twenty-four when I began to see that the life I had was one I had created. Before that, I believed there was just something wrong with me, that I wasn't valuable. I started believing this at age five while trying to go to sleep hungry in a crappy, run-down, single-wide trailer. Once I planted the belief, I found a lot of evidence to prove everything was somehow my fault because I wasn't valuable. When my stepfather touched me inappropriately, I didn't tell my mom. I was sure it was my fault. When we were living in our car, I didn't tell anyone in our extended family. Somehow it was my fault because I wasn't valuable. By eighteen, after four different families, and I thought maybe it was because there was something wrong with me.

In college, I continued to believe I wasn't valuable. It wasn't a conscious thought, though. The conscious thought was, this feels good, so I should do it. Getting drunk was fun, and sleeping around was fun for a moment. But afterward, when I was lying in bed, I felt like crap. Just like I did in that crappy, run-down trailer.

After getting married and having my first child, I longed to feel valuable and okay, but I didn't know how. I joined Mary Kay Cosmetics. I began to work hard. I thought if I won my car, then I would be okay. I visualized winning the car, I visualized my car party, but I forgot to visualize feeling better about myself. Even after winning the car, at night I still didn't feel valuable.

Then I thought, if I could become a director, then I would be okay. I did that twelve months later, and I still wasn't okay. I had helped two other people win their cars. My favorite part of being a director was teaching people how to work on their self-esteem issues. Ironically, I still didn't feel valuable and my self-esteem was in the toilet. I thought accomplishments would make me feel better. Nothing worked until I changed my opinion about myself.

Your behavior can be a powerful indicator light for the negative beliefs you have about yourself. Let's look at overeating. What if you overeat because you want to use the layers of fat to keep people at a distance? What if you overeat because you don't think you are valuable and worthy of love, so food fills the insatiable need for love?

Maybe overeating isn't your issue? What about drinking too much? Do you drink because you've had a rough day and you need to relax? Do you drink to excess so you can and do socially unacceptable behavior, like flirt with people you aren't married to or say what you really think?

This is not about judgment. This is about being intentional, living a self-examined life, and understanding the "why" behind what we do and how we act.

So how do you fix it? For starters, you don't fix it. You begin by accepting your whole self—flaws and all. By accepting yourself, you begin to make it safe for your mind and heart to tell you the truth. If you are filled with self-judgment, then your brain may actually try to hide the truth from you out of fear that you will berate yourself. This may seem very strange. You've heard the expression, "you are your own worst enemy." Why do we do that? Judge not, lest you be judged. That means don't judge yourself. Love your neighbor as you love yourself. How can you love others if you don't love yourself?

If my friends say terrible things about themselves, I will often say, "Don't talk about my friend that way." It's like defending someone against themselves. We may think negative self-talk is productive because it drives us or motivates us. Really, it erodes our self-esteem.

For the next three days, whenever you have a negative encounter with someone else—your boss, your spouse, your friend—write down the behavior that started the negative encounter. Did your roommate leave socks on the floor? Did your coworker not greet you when you came in to work? Then take some time each day to review the list and, one by one, get very curious about why that interaction was negative. What was the thought you had after the behavior happened? What feeling did you experience after you had that thought?

For the moment, we are just exploring and getting curious. In the next chapter, we're going to unpack self-awareness and conflicting values. I find that conflicting values explain over half my negative interactions.

You may feel frustrated that we are simply writing down these interactions, feelings, and thoughts and not solving anything. Here's my answer to that: The solution lies in fully understanding the problem. Often a clearly defined equation is easy to solve. However, a murky, awkward, unknown issue is nearly impossible to unravel. Begin to get comfortable being uncomfortable.

The greatest pollution problem we face today is negativity. Eliminate the negative attitude and believe you can do anything. Replace 'if I can, I hope, maybe' with 'I can, I will, I must.
- Mary Kay Ash

Impossible is just a word thrown around by small men who find it easier to live in the world they've been given than to explore the power they have to change it. Impossible is not a fact. It's an opinion. Impossible is potential. Impossible is temporary. Impossible is nothing.
– Muhammad Ali

You measure the size of the accomplishment by the obstacles you have to overcome to reach your goals.
- Booker T. Washington

Self-awareness: Assess the Situation

Self-awareness is not self-centeredness, and spirituality is not narcissism. 'Know thyself' is not a narcissistic pursuit.
- Marianne Williamson

On New Year's Day 2016, Barry and I decided to join my friend's annual Black-Eyed Pea 5K. The 5K is free, but you can make a donation to the local track team. After the run, my friend serves black-eyed peas (supposedly good luck for the New Year). I had taught a goal-setting workshop a few days before, symbolically for us, we decided to run the 5K to demonstrate our commitment to getting healthier. No training, just decided to go run 3.2 miles. After completing the race, we decided to complete one 5K per month for the whole year.

The next month we chose a race in Tulsa, two hours away from where we live. We had to register for the race, find a hotel, let our kids know we'd be out of town, get into Tulsa early enough for packet pickup, and decide where we wanted dinner the night before the race. It took a lot more planning than rolling out of bed, putting on warm clothes, and driving across town to a free race at my friend's house. Both were timed races, but each required a different commitment.

As you begin your journey, we need to assess what level of commitment you will need for the journey. Some areas may be as simple as rolling out of bed and putting on tennis shoes. Others may involve a lot more planning and preparation. You may not get to control the circumstances you encounter, but you get to control how you encounter the circumstance.

Notice Your Interactions

Self-awareness is essential to Be Freaking Awesome and to improving your relationships. When you first begin to be more self-aware, it may be exhausting. It involves noticing every interaction you have and assessing whether the inter-action is positive or negative. If you aren't aware that you are hurting someone's feelings, you can't look at the beliefs that caused that behavior. If you don't realize you are not listening to your kids when they talk, then you can't improve commu-nication with them. In the movie What Women Want, Mel Gibson's character thinks everyone loves him and thinks he's amazing. But when he can hear women's thoughts, he realizes how obtuse he is and how people think he is a self-centered, pompous jerk. We won't be able to hear people's thoughts, but we can notice situations that don't go the way we think they should. I call it living an examined life.

To increase your self-awareness, it's a good idea to spend a few minutes at the end of each day reviewing the day's inter-actions. Did you have conflict? Were you the one upset or were you involved with someone else's emotions? Did you have conversations with people you care about? Were they mean-ingful or simply about superficial things like weather, sports, and news? It takes a lot of courage to review your behavior and interactions to find patterns. When I first began the process of being more self-aware, I had to keep a notebook. I would write down interactions, negative behavior, and negative emotions I experienced. As time goes on, I'm less likely to write down interactions, but I still spend time (especially alone time in the car) reviewing interactions to see how I can improve my communication and my responses.

Also, begin to notice the things people say to you, maybe even in a teasing way. For instance, after you share an opinion at work, if someone routinely says, "Well, tell me how you really feel." Perhaps that is an indicator, sort of like a check engine light, that you were very direct and perhaps hurt someone's feelings.

This process is about noticing your behavior so you can decide if you like the person you are and if you are closer to developing the character traits you want to have.

Your self-awareness exercise is to keep a journal for the next fourteen days. Notice your interactions with others. Rate your interactions with friends, family, and coworkers. Are they pleasant? Do you go deep with at least some people in your life? What about work? Do you ever have conflict? What are the interactions like? Try to get curious about some of the root causes. If nothing comes up in that time frame, think about the last time you were with a large group of people and it didn't go well. Perhaps the family reunion or Thanksgiving at Grandma's house. What were the interactions like?

When you have negative situations and unpleasant interactions, sometimes we have a tendency to say, "Here it goes again. I will never learn. Why do I always say the wrong thing?" On and on, we beat ourselves up. Instead, what if you looked at each negative interaction as a way to learn and improve? If you don't become aware of issues, you can't improve them or correct the negative beliefs that cause these behaviors.

One particularly helpful way to begin this practice is to simply notice when you feel angry and upset. Immediately express your gratitude that you are now more consciously aware of something, even if you aren't sure what it is yet that you are aware of. You're moving forward on the journey and making progress.

Developing Emotional Muscles

When you are working to achieve your goals and live a remarkable life, it's sort of like building muscles by going to the gym. When you first start working out, you may only be able to lift ten pounds and do ten repetitions. As you continue to exercise, you will increase the number of repetitions and the amount of weight you can lift. Your muscles get stronger with each workout.

My daughter Sami broke her ankle when she was in the eighth grade. After surgery, she was on crutches for two weeks and then in a walking boot for six weeks. She did this over Thanksgiving break, and we wondered if she would be in shape before soccer season started in March. What we found is that her muscles in the broken leg had atrophied. Her left leg was visibly smaller than her right leg. Without use, her muscles began to shrink and weaken. She returned to soccer, but only because she was the goalie and didn't have to run all the time.

Emotional muscles are also weak when you first start to use them. When we get hurt, often instead of stopping to heal (get stitches), we put a thin layer of "concrete" over the crack in our heart. When we get hurt again, we put another layer of concrete over the crack. Often this layer of concrete has a vow with it that says, I never want to feel hurt ever again. By making this vow or promise and limiting our willingness to feel pain, we also limit our ability to feel joy, love, and other positive feelings.

Self-awareness is a muscle. The more it is used, the stronger it will get. When I was in college, my nickname was Queen B. It didn't stand for beautiful. I would say to people, "You may not like me. But I will get this done, and it will be amazing. I'm not in this so you'll like me." To a large degree, I didn't care what people thought of me—to a fault. I was an officer with a student organization, and my advisor had to sit me down several times to explain to me that there were more effective ways to accomplish things, ways that didn't involve hurting people's feelings.

While still in college, I joined Mary Kay Cosmetics. Nothing like a career in sales and recruiting to knock the rough edges off. In Mary Kay, the feedback loop was much faster. If I didn't effectively communicate, people didn't buy products from me or return my calls. I also had a senior director whom I adored and who was very nurturing to me, but a lot of the people on my team found her to be overbearing and too pushy. Watching her interact provided a negative example of what not to do. At the same time, our relationship helped me begin to build my self-awareness muscle. I found her directness refreshing.

I'm still a direct person. I'm still very task oriented and love to finish big projects on time. However, now I see that if all I do is run over people I won't have a team to work with. I make a great effort to be inclusive and have learned to slow down to communicate. Those who work with me are probably rolling on the floor laughing right now, because they have a front-row seat when I don't get my way and become frustrated.

When I was developing these self-awareness muscles, I had to say a lot of chants in my head to remind me of my goal to build people. "People are more important than a task." "No one remembers what you know, they remember how you made them feel." Or "They don't care what you know unless they know that you care."

There are a variety of paths to developing emotional muscles. Remember how we talked about planting the garden and choosing if we wanted tomatoes or cucumbers? Can you imagine how hard it would be to plant a garden in concrete? Our job is to excavate the concrete, find the wounds, and allow them to heal.

For me, I had to seek professional counseling to do this excavation work. For some of you, professional counseling may be extremely beneficial. For others, you may be able to process this with a trusted friend.

Grace for Yourself

In addition to becoming self-aware about how we treat others, we need to be aware of how we treat ourselves. Are you kind in how you speak to yourself? One of the worst things you can do to yourself, besides lying, is to beat yourself up. When I evaluate my self-talk, I often realize that the things I am saying to myself I wouldn't say to my worst enemy.

You are an idiot.

Why didn't you think of that?

How could you be so stupid?

I can't believe I did that.

When are you ever going to learn?

And worse.

You have to become aware to treat yourself with kindness. Often when I'm talking with someone, they will say things about themselves much like the negative list above. That's when I tell them to "please stop talking about my friend that way." It helps me to think of myself as a friend. I imagine someone saying the things I say to myself to one of my friends. I would be upset with that person for being an insensitive, not affirming, and an overall mean person. Why is it okay to say these things to ourselves if we wouldn't say them to another human?

When you have grace for yourself, you also create grace for others. As you become more aware of the things you say to yourself, I believe you will become more aware of what you say to others. I was talking with someone about why her child had random outbursts and started yelling in anger. Then I rode with this person in the car during traffic and watched her have random outbursts and start yelling at the other drivers. She had never put it together that her child was mimicking what she was doing. That was the most frustrating parenting lesson I've learned. My youngest would sometimes go from zero to crazy person in 4.2 seconds. I couldn't figure out this behavior. But one day she couldn't find her shoes. I calmly asked her if she looked here or there. Then I suddenly got really frustrated and went from zero to crazy person in 4.2 seconds. AHHHHH. She was doing what I did. If I wanted her to stay calm, then I had to stay calm.

Notice Everything—Good, Bad, Neutral

As you are on this journey, you might have figured out that I think you should notice everything. When things go well, I want you to write them in a success journal. When things go poorly, I want you to consider why, to get curious about the negative encounters. And even when things are neutral, observe why that is. If you get into the habit of noticing everything, you are well on your way to living a self-examined life. But that's not all. When you notice things, you also begin to develop empathy. Let's say that you make a comment that you think is neutral or positive, and the person reacts negatively. You get to stop and think, did I say that in a tone that can be construed as negative? Was I communicating clearly? Then, if you feel like you in fact have a clear conscience, you can begin to be curious about the other person and why that triggered them.

There are two different ways we can think about a person who has given us a negative response. We can think that person is a jerk, assigning a judgment based on our perception of his character. Or, we can think that person must be having a bad day. In this scenario, we give the person grace based on our perception of his circumstances. In parenting, we are encouraged to think about how children are characterized. Meaning if they typically are kind and respectful, then we may give them more leeway or treat their misbehavior as an exception and react appropriately. However, if every single day you have issues with disrespect or dishonesty, then you react differently, because up to this point they are characterized by this behavior.

I was talking with a recent college graduate. She shared that they couldn't figure out why they were discouraged and blue, crying themselves to sleep each night. I shared that I have had several college graduates go from part time to full time, and the first August after they graduated they got really down, unmotivated, and less creative. After this happened a couple of times, I realized that the transition from child to adult happens gradually during college for most, but the harsh reality of going to work every single day, day after day after day, hits people differently and represents the final transition to adulthood. It can result in mourning, and if you aren't careful you can get stuck in the mourning and end up depressed for a year or more.

Self-awareness about what you're feeling and why will keep you moving on the journey. It may also prevent you from making unwise choices to meet try to alleviate bad feelings.

Identify Good or Unpleasant

For me, I want to live a life full of adventure, peace, and reacting calmly and in a healthy way to everything that happens to me. For me, peace is figuring out how my words and actions are perceived by others. This is a tricky thing because there's a fine balance between worrying about what others think and making sure you are the kind of person who creates peace. For me, any situation that results in my anger is categorized as unpleasant. Situations where I am able to stand up for myself without tearing someone else down or getting angry, I classify as healthy. In every encounter I have, I want to be the person who brings strong, positive energy. I want to be the person who makes everyone feel better. There are days I fail at a very high level. I get frustrated easily, I am quickly angered, I yell, I cuss, I snap, and then I beat myself up about it. This is because my behavior is in conflict with my values of being strong with positive energy.

When you look at your encounters, when is your behavior in conflict with your values? Do you weirdly enjoy getting into arguments with the people in your life? Or do you hate the feelings left over after conflict? It's important to tune in to your interactions to consider how you can be stronger, healthier, and more peaceful in your life. When you look at these interactions and decide how you want to be, incorporate them into your vision of your ideal life.

Conflicting Values

While noticing your interactions, you may stumble upon situations where it doesn't seem clear cut if the interaction is positive or negative. For instance, I have a value that I want to be "for me" while creating win-win-win scenarios with the people I interact with. I also have a value that I want to be a supportive wife. There are times when I feel that I can't carry out both of these values at the same time. If I am on autopilot, my human nature is to protect myself and be for me at the expense of everyone else. As long as the support my husband needs allows me to feel in control (not a value I hold, but one that I work to get rid of), then I can easily be supportive. There are times when I have to stop and ask myself, how can I support him and be for me? How can I create the win-win-win?

My brain works fast; I see patterns and connections and logistics quickly. I also think a lot. I have a tendency to present an idea and expect that my husband, who is also my business partner, will just get on board with it instantly. I have had to learn that it's not fair to expect him to see the connections I see without giving him time to think, or at least for me to take the time to explain it slowly and rationally. Luckily, my husband also thinks fast, but he is naturally wired to find the potholes in an idea. So, while he's working through all the potholes he's found, I get frustrated. Finally, after twenty-three years of marriage, I'm learning to give him a bit of time to noodle the idea, work out the details for himself, and come to his own conclusions. He's also had to learn that just because there's going to be a pothole in the road doesn't mean we shouldn't go down that path. It means we can use his ability to create a plan of how we will go over, around, and through the possible problems.

I first discovered the concept of conflicting values years ago when I was in angst about whether we should go to Toronto for Canada Day (July 1). My husband is Canadian, and his dad throws a huge party every year for Canada Day, allowing us to see most of our Canadian family in one long weekend. However, we had a goal to beef up our savings account. I was talking to my best friend, wondering why this was causing me so much angst. Finally, I realized that I value my children's relationship with their extended family. As adults, we're able to talk on the phone, connect via social media, or even write letters and emails, but kids need to be with family if they are going to get to know them. This value was in conflict with another value: our goal of being financially stable. Once I realized that I had two different values in conflict, I could change my strategy of how to solve the problem and stop my emotional turmoil. I decided that older family members won't live forever, but I could make more money. In this instance, the trip was more important than the savings account. However, that also meant that on a day-to-day basis I had to make wise financial decisions, like not eating out, in order to maintain that value of being financially stable. I couldn't always choose to make financial security second; otherwise, it wasn't an actual value.

"It's not your fault that you are screwed up.
It's your fault if you stay screwed up."
- Jen Sincero

During this journey, besides self-awareness, another important skill is self-belief. When we are born, we are fearless. We believe we can do anything, have all our needs met, and are completely lovable. Then we grow, mature, and become adults. During that time of growth and maturity, we learn to be careful—don't get hurt, you may not be able to climb that high, boys don't cry, girls don't like math and science, and whatever else our parents believe we need to be prepared for life. Jen Sincero, author and motivational speaker, says, "It's not your fault that you are screwed up. It's your fault if you stay screwed up." I have found that forgiving others for the things they have said or done to me, while hard, is much easier than forgiving myself for the stupid decisions I made that caused me pain. Or worse, the decisions I made because I was still wounded from a previous injury.

I Am Enough

Another concept Jack Canfield teaches is "I Am Enough." From my perspective, one assessment you can do to determine if you need to work on self-esteem is to look yourself in the mirror and say, "I am enough." Say it again. Can you say it five times in a row easily without flinching? I couldn't. It was super hard, I felt like I was lying to myself. I followed Jack's advice and said it in the mirror five times in a row morning and night for twenty-one days. By the end, it got a whole lot easier.

If you don't have any issues with this, give yourself a big high-five and a pat on the back. If you found it hard, your homework today is to look yourself in the eye (in the mirror) and lovingly say, "I am enough."

Evaluate Your Character Traits

As you look at the list of character traits you want to develop and how you want to live your designed life, you first have to assess your current situation and determine what level of planning and commitment the different areas will take.

For instance, if you decide you want to be debt free, the first step in this process is to gather all your current debt statements, make a list of how much money you owe each creditor, and come up with a total. This is an assessment. I recommend taking that one step further. I encourage you to review those debt statements and see how you got into debt. Did you spend the money intentionally? Or did you add to your credit cards with things you didn't really need or eating out when you really couldn't afford it?

Now, look at the character traits you want to possess. Will any of those character traits help you in the process of paying off debt. Could you pay off the debt with just a little diligence? Do you need to exercise self-control? Are you looking to add perseverance? Can you see how paying off debt, whether a little or a lot, could help you develop perseverance? I believe if you can tie in how you want to live your life with the character traits you want to develop, the effort you put in will be magnified.

I have been a part of the direct sales industry off and on for over twenty years. Many times I offered the product or business opportunity to someone and they rejected my offer. This could feel like a failure, however, if I'm trying to develop perseverance this rejection actually gets me closer to that goal.

We joke in our family that you should never pray for patience. The logic is that the best way to develop patience is to be in situations that require you to be patient. Therefore, praying for patience could invite situations where you will build the character trait of patience.

The next time you are dealing with a difficult situation, consider what character traits you are developing in the process.

Our deepest fear is not that we are inadequate.
Our deepest fear is that we are powerful
beyond measure.

Self-aware as a Parent

I read an article that said, moms get angry when they don't get their way. Wait ... what? You mean children, right? Nope, moms. I began to notice, and it's really true, at least in my life. God often uses my children as a mirror to show me the areas that still need work.

Becoming self-aware as a parent of teenagers is a little tricky. Primarily because most anything you say can and will be used against you in the court of their minds. I believe being self-aware during this critical stage of their growth is a major contributor to the long-term health of your relationship. As a parent of a teenager, I hope empathy is on your list of character traits that you want to develop.

If you can, think back to your teenage years and remember how hard everything could be and then imagine how you would have wanted your parents to handle it. Every child is different, but some of the best advice I've heard is that the teenage years are a time when we need to begin to trust our kids and give them more responsibility, letting them learn with a safety net. Once they leave your house, the mistakes they make can have long-term consequences, so they need opportunities to make mistakes that can more easily be fixed.

To do this, trust must be established and maintained, and communication must remain open. Sometimes I think people expect their teenagers to mess up, and then when they do, parents say, "See, I told you so." What if we flipped that? What if we believed the very best about them?

I think this principle of believing the best of someone also applies to other relationships. If you expect people to mess up and disappoint you, they will. If you expect that everyone is doing the best they can with the tools and information they have, you are right. Do you want people to believe you are going to disappoint them? Or would you rather they believe that you are doing the best you can, and if you could do better you would? I believe that the world would be a better place if we all assumed the best about people.

Now that you're on the road to self-awareness, we'll discuss the roadblocks you may encounter in the next chapter.

The only thing standing between you and your goal is the bulls**t story you keep telling yourself as to why you can't achieve it.
- Jordan Belfort

Every human has four endowments - self awareness, conscience, independent will and creative imagination. These give us the ultimate human freedom... The power to choose, to respond, to change.
- Stephen Covey

Roadblocks You Might Encounter

*Obstacles are those frightful things you see
when you take your eyes off your goal.*
- Henry Ford

I was adopted as a child. I've met many other adults who were adopted as children. Even if you know in your head that your life is better because you were adopted (I would have died in a trailer fire), you still wrestle with feelings of abandonment. Mine was compounded by my adopted mom dying of cancer. Even though it's not logical, it still feels like being abandoned.

As you begin the journey of healing, you will have setbacks. It's important you know this going in. Oftentimes, you may be the only person who knows you have a setback. As humans, we are very good pretenders. We can even fool ourselves. One of the gifts you can give to yourself is to be completely honest with yourself. I have often been frustrated with people who lie to themselves. Sometimes being honest with ourselves is the most painful experience. When we delude ourselves and live in denial, it feels less painful, but it's really killing a part of our heart. Remember, guard your heart above all else for it is the wellspring of life. In the stories you tell yourself, how do you figure out if you are being honest or deluding yourself? Our challenging life situations, including adoption, can sometimes throw up roadblocks on our journey to be awesome.

Shame—the Ultimate Roadblock

When you take stock of the roadblocks, you may encounter voices in your head telling you that you can't do this. You can't make the necessary changes, you can't_____ (fill in the blank). I'm not saying that you are schizophrenic: I am saying that you may be your own worst enemy in this process.

To be a person that you want to hang around, first pause to listen to the voices. What are they saying? Often these voices are communicating shame. There is a difference between shame and guilt. According to Brené Brown, author of Daring Greatly, Rising Strong and other excellent books, guilt says, I did something wrong. Shame says, there's something wrong with me.

Often the messages from childhood turn into soundtracks in our head. As I child, I overheard people talking about me as a kid. They would say, "Oh, bless her heart, she'll never amount to anything. She'll probably end up just like her mother." "If she graduates high school and doesn't end up on drugs, it will be a miracle." People didn't mean to be putting limiting beliefs on me. In their limited experience, anyone who had experienced as much trauma as I had, was pretty much a lost cause.

These years also came with a lot of shame. "There must be something wrong with me; no one wants to keep me." "No matter how hard I try, it's never good enough." And my favorite, "I don't know if they want you or the social security check that comes with you." That will mess up your perception of money for a good long time.

Eventually, I learned that the very best thing to happen to me was living in four families. I learned that each family has different rules and norms. This meant that as an adult, I got to set my own rules and norms. I didn't have the belief that there is one way things have to be done because I'd seen four different versions of how things were done. It taught me incredible sales skills. I had to learn the different personalities and figure out how to get my needs met. More importantly, I didn't have twenty years of the same negative habits and ruts in my brain from experiencing the same thing over and over again. At most, I only experienced one family's dysfunction for about five years.

In my 2015 trip to the World Championship of Public Speaking, I used a gardening analogy. You have to pull out the weeds in the garden of your mind, and if you don't pull them out by the root, they will just come right back. Nature abhors a vacuum, so removing the weed isn't enough. You also have to plant a new seed. A new thought that will lead to the life and character traits you've decided you want.

Lack of Motivation

Sometimes, you know what you need to do, you know why you want to do it, and yet you still don't feel like doing it. You feel like sitting on the couch and binge-watching Netflix. We think we'll feel better after resting, but then after six hours we feel worse. Probably because in the "I don't feel like it" emotional state, we make unhealthy choices, so even the stuff we binge-watch is trash. The food we choose may be terrible for our bodies. We know better. Why don't we do it?

I think there are a variety of reasons for our lack of motivation. This is when we need to give our self-awareness muscle a great workout. We have to get curious about why we "don't feel like it." We have to ask ourselves, what is going on here? Sometimes we legitimately need to rest. I am a recovering perfectionist, and I love a very full schedule. That means I have to schedule downtime. When I do, my mental chatter while I'm resting isn't as bad. What's interesting is that sometimes after the much-needed rest I beat myself up and say things like, "Do you know how much stuff you could have gotten done during that nap?" I've learned I have to set a goal and a reward. For instance, on the weekends, even though we have a housekeeper who cleans the basics, there are inevitably projects lurking about. We have found that we have to say, if we get the laundry caught up, the garage cleaned, and a couple of naps in, we're going to feel good about this weekend. Then on Sunday night when the mental chatter starts, I'm able to say to myself, "Nope, I decided that garage, laundry, and nap were on the agenda. Yay me for getting it done."

How do you combat a lack of motivation? Start. Commit to spending twenty minutes a day on something toward your goal. If your goal is to be a more kind and well-balanced person, what book can you read or TED talk (www.TED.com) can you watch that will get you a bit closer to that goal. Is there a podcast that you can subscribe to that will help you think differently?

In the next chapter, we're going to talk about addressing fear. Some of the lack of motivation is rooted in fear, fear of success or fear of failure. I love the Marianne Williamson quote, "Our deepest fear is not that we are inadequate. Our deepest fear is that we are powerful beyond measure." If we really go for it, who will we be? If we pretend to be tired, sick, or busy, we can have a great excuse for not becoming our whole self. Our goals can wait for years for the laundry, soccer practice, or the latest episode of our favorite show. Then we wonder why we get more and more cranky and less and less motivated. We aren't living life to the fullest.

Outside Influences

When you decide to change or grow, you will naturally want to share with the people you love. Sometimes these people will have opinions about what you are doing or what you are attempting to do. They may even decide that they don't like what you are doing, that they don't like you changing. If you have been codependent and waited on your kids hand and foot, but suddenly decide to raise children who are responsible and able to take care of themselves, your children may not like this. If your friend is accustomed to being able to call you and dump all her problems on you, but you decide that you want to limit your exposure to negative people and experiences, your friend isn't going to like this.

Dealing with this sort of reaction can be tough. Simply express gratitude for them sharing their opinion, and then leave it with them. Objectively look at what they are sharing, and decide if there's any truth or any value to what they are saying. Often, they are expressing their own fears and discomfort. Your transformative journey could trigger them to look at their own life, and they may not want to do that. In the case of your children, you will have to be strong, kind, and committed. If you feel yourself getting weak, think of a person who has the character qualities your children will possess because you give them everything they ask for and wait on them. Perhaps you know someone who is an overgrown two-year-old, and she throw tantrums to get her way all the time. Do you want your kids to turn out like that? If you don't want your children to be permanently dependent on you with no sense of responsibility, begin now to guide them in how to be less selfish. Stop enabling them.

As you look at your current life and compare it to the life you want, you may notice things that don't belong anymore. Jim Rohn, a famous motivational speaker, once said you become like the five people you spend the most time with. As you begin your journey to Be Freaking Awesome, there may be people in your life who don't support this journey. I have a theory on why. Most people like the status quo. When you begin a journey of change for the better, it can be threatening to others or may make them feel uncomfortable about the rut they are traveling through. They also may be happy being unhappy.

Have you ever met people who if they didn't have something to complain about they wouldn't know how to carry on a conversation?

As you begin this journey, consider the people who consume most of your discretionary time. Do these people build you up, tear you down, encourage your dreams, or rain on every parade? If you discover that the people you spend the most time with are negative and tear you down, it may be time to limit your exposure. If this person is a spouse or a coworker, the situation gets tricky. If you eat in the breakroom at lunch, and everyone who eats in there complains the whole time, you may have to eat lunch outside or in your car. Next, find four other people you can spend time with to offset the time you spend with the person who is negative. If you don't have four people, then it is time to begin to make new friends. You may have to begin to volunteer with organizations that put you in contact with people who have values that match yours.

I'm not saying ditch every friend who isn't 100 percent positive all the time. I'm saying that while you are going through this growth period you may need to be extra careful about people who aren't supportive of your journey. When you get stronger and more confident in this new way of being, you may be able to spend time with people who are negative without it dragging you down. Be gentle with yourself during this time of growth.

What Are You Willing to Give Up?

Besides spending time with negative people, there may be other things you have to give up. You may have to give up the need to make people happy and worry about what others will think of you. I recommend that if you are doing something that someone doesn't approve of, look at that person's life. Does he have the character traits and relationships that you want? Then you might take his approval under advisement. If he is miserable, lacks character, and doesn't have strong healthy relationships, then his opinion of what you're doing might not really matter. I love the quote, "It's none of your business what other people think of you."

What kind of TV shows and movies do you watch? How much TV do you watch? I think it's interesting when people love to watch scary movies, horror movies, or worse—the news—all the time and then can't figure out why they struggle with anxiety. Essentially, if you become like the five people you spend the most time with and if watching the news consumes more time than some of your relationships, then the news has become one of your five people. It's easy to see why you might be anxious since the news is often negative. That's what sells.

Recently, we cut the cord and got rid of cable. Instead, we have a Roku device with subscriptions to Netflix and Hulu. I still watch TV, but now on my terms.. Also, my favorite thing is that it's now super easy to watch TED Talks because it is just an app on my Roku device. If you have a long journey of things you want to change in your life or if you want to start a new business, you may have to give up watching TV altogether for a while. Seth Godin in his book, *Leap First* says, "If you want to start a side hustle, read more books or write a book, don't tell me you don't have time and then spend two to three hours a day in front of the television." Ouch.

Other things you may have to give up

Excuses. Jen Sincero says, "If you really want to change your life, you'll find a way. If you aren't committed, you'll find excuses." What are your favorite excuses? Make a list and eliminate them.

Eating poorly. If your body needs to be a well-oiled machine, then why fill it full of fried foods and wonder why you don't have the energy to chase your dreams.

Complaining about your life. The best way to immediately have a better life is to express gratitude for everything in it. Everything. If you have debt, then express gratitude that the process of getting out of debt will teach you diligence and self-control. The Law of Attraction says that whatever you talk about the most with the most passion is what you will get more of. That means when you complain loudly and often about anything, you will get more of it. How frightening is that?

Perfectionism. Brené Brown says that perfectionism is rooted in shame. If you aren't perfect, what will people think? I'll tell you, they'll think you are real. If they don't, you may want to rethink if that person gets to be one of the five people in your life.

A clean house. I have heard people say, "I can't hire a housekeeper because I can't find one that meets my standards." Really? A clean house doesn't make you money. A clean house doesn't prove you are a good mom or wife. A clean house doesn't guarantee a good marriage. I would encourage you to figure out what needs are being met by having a clean house "to your standards." I have found that visual clutter is distracting to me and I like a tidy house. I like a clean kitchen when I go to bed. So, I hired a housekeeper, and I try to have the kitchen clean when I go to bed. Reasonable expectations, not perfectionistic expectations.

Your kids getting perfect grades. Are your expectations for your child building your relationship or causing conflict? I am baffled by how many people jeopardize long-term relationships with their children for the sake of straight A's. Think back to your high-school grades. Do they affect you today? Is your life better or worse based on the grades you received? Do you want long-term strong relationships with your kids? Then think through the expectations you have, and draw a line out ten years to see where this is going to end up.

Do you have their heart?

Do they trust you to tell them the hard stuff? I know it's

cliché to say that kids spell love T-I-M-E, but how can you get to know them and their heart without spending time with them?

What's your list? What do you need to give up to go up? If your hand is clenched around how things are now, you can't receive the blessings in store for you. Make a list of all the things you currently have in your life and mind that don't contribute to a level 10 life. Will this thing, idea, or belief help you Be Freaking Awesome? If not, get rid of it.

Consistency

Consistency is a tricky word for me. In my head, I know that if one drop of water drips on the same spot of concrete over and over again, the consistent water drip will break up the concrete. Our actions are the same way. If I do one thing over and over again, I can accomplish anything. I think I am learning that I can't tell myself I'm going to be consistent; I have to trick my brain into thinking it's a short-term thing and then renew the commitment later.

In Alcoholics Anonymous, they say that you can't quit drinking for the rest of your life. It's not possible. It's too much for your brain to handle. They recommend that you quit drinking today. Then tomorrow, you can decide again. You string together enough days and next thing you know you have one year sober under your belt. The more days you don't drink, the easier it gets to not drink—that day.

I even struggled reading the book called *The Power of Consistency*. I only read it because my friend, Viki, who doesn't typically read self-help books, was reading it, and she thought I'd like it because I love personal development. What I have learned is that while I don't love the word, I do know the concept of consistency is important. I know that my kids are more balanced if I'm consistent in my love, my discipline, my rules, and my fun-loving side. I know that when it comes to paying off lots debt, consistency will solve the problem.

Healing Is Like an Onion

When you peel an onion, each layer is separate. It can stand alone, and it protects the inner layers. Sometimes when people begin a journey of healing, they are only aware of an outer-layer problem. As they peel back that problem and examine it to find the root cause, they may think that is the only healing they need, and it may very well be. I honestly believe God will only give us what we can handle. I think if we had to try to heal all our wounds at the same time, God would have to put us in a drug-induced coma because we wouldn't be able to handle that concentration of pain.

The way some people walk around not healing from their emotional pain is like they have a giant gaping cut and won't get stitches. They swear it doesn't hurt. I would love to believe them and just let them go on their merry way, but most of the time they are making a mess by "emotionally bleeding" on others everywhere they go. When you get the cut stitched up, it hurts, but it heals. I have several scars on my body from places where I've had to get stitches before. Most of the time, these scars don't hurt. They have healed; they may leave a mark on my body, and I have a story. But it doesn't hurt anymore.

This is the way it is with emotional healing. We have to stop and take time to either bandage the wound or get stitches. This process may involve needing pain medication, antidepressants, or anti-anxiety medication.

As Sandra Wilson says, "Hurt people, hurt people." When people first get started healing, it can seem so overwhelming. Everywhere you find something new that you need to address. It can feel like your entire life is a complete mess. The most important thing to remember is that as long as you don't quit, you can't fail. Getting healthy is a journey you will pursue as long as you are breathing.

Life is the journey of pursuing health. It is an ongoing endeavor. I hope you will keep going in spite of the roadblocks.

Address the Fears

Courage is not the absence of fear, but rather the judgment that something else is more important than fear. - Ambrose Redmoon

Over the years, I've come to divide fear into categories. First, there is fear based on actual experiences you have encountered. The second category of fear is irrational fear, and the final category is subconscious fear.

Fear Based in Reality

When we are small children, we are taught to fear hot stoves. We may have even touched a hot stove accidentally and know that it hurts. It is rational to have a healthy respect for hot stoves. It would be irrational to decide that you are never going to cook again because stoves could burn you.

When we drink hot chocolate or coffee and we burn our tongue, we don't think that we should never drink hot beverages again. We learn and adjust our behavior. We may allow the beverage to cool. We may blow on the drink to cool it faster. We may not care. We don't stop drinking hot chocolate out of fear of burning our tongue, right?

Yet sometimes other experiences cause us to completely change our lives out of fear of pain. The one that comes to mind is people who have been hurt at church. I call them church toast, burnt on both sides. Perhaps they were in a situation where they were judged, ridiculed, ostracized, abandoned, or just plain mistreated. Church is full of humans, and many of those humans are hurting. Hurt people, hurt people. It is very tragic, and it often results in people leaving the church and never returning. This makes me very sad.

I went through a phase where I didn't like church. I hadn't been hurt. No one had done a single thing wrong; I just wasn't happy. I tried to go because I knew it was good for my children, and the rest of my family loved our church. I loved the people in my church, but I just wasn't satisfied. I honestly believe there was nothing the church could have done differently.

I learned to embrace the feeling of not liking church. Prior to this phase, I had been deliriously happy with our church. The people truly were our family, and we loved serving. People would share their story of not liking church or being so hurt in church that they didn't want to go back. I couldn't relate. I don't think I judged them, but I had no point of reference to compare and feel empathy. After I went through this season of being unsatisfied, I could relate so much more easily. I could really empathize, and I was less likely to inadvertently give them a pat religious answer.

What is sad to me is that sometimes people don't push through the pain to find another church. It's like they decided to never drink hot chocolate again because they burned their tongue once. I'm not trying to say the pain you feel from rejection at church is as inconsequential as a burn on the tongue. But you may be missing out on blessing in your avoidance of pain.

You may also live in a place where there aren't options to find another faith community. I know someone who lived in a small town, and he had to drive an hour each way to find a church that was loving and supportive, while teaching actual truth. His spiritual growth was worth the two-hour commute.

What other areas of your life have you decided to never do or try again because you were hurt before? Was unforgiveness on your list of character traits? I doubt it, so consider forgiving the situation and trying to find another way to re-engage.

Irrational Fear

Mark Twain said, "I've lived through some terrible things in my life, some of which actually happened." Many of the fears we have are made up, the monster in the closet cementing us to our beds. Irrational fear is fear that is contrived and has no basis in actual experience. This fear is very difficult to overcome because it isn't based in logic. Nevertheless, it can feel very real.

Remember the clever acronym for fear is:

False | Evidence | Appearing | Real

We have to confront the evidence and use logic to overcome the irrational. I have found the most effective way to do this is to write out your thoughts. If you can write them down, you can begin to see the irrationality of them.

What's the Worst Thing That Can Happen?

Somewhere on my journey, I learned to apply the "What's the worst thing that can happen?" logic to my fears. When my daughter Sami was four, she took a tumbling class. She was trying to learn how to do the uneven bars, which I think for the four-year-old class was simply swinging around one on your belly. She decided that she was too afraid to go on them. I walked her through the "What's the worst thing that can happen?" (Yes, she was four.)

Mom: What's the worst thing that can happen if you get on the uneven bars?

Sami: I could fall.

Mom: If you fall, what's the worst thing that can happen?

Sami: I could hit my head.

Mom: If you hit your head, what's the worst thing that can happen?

Sami: I could have to go to the hospital.

Mom: If you go to the hospital, what's the worst thing that can happen?

Sami: I could have to have a test or scan of my head.

Mom: If you have a scan of your head, what's the worst thing that can happen?

Sami: Uh, I don't know.

Mom: Well, do you think you might die?

Sami: No, you probably wouldn't let me do something that might kill me.

Mom: Would you break something?

Sami: Maybe.

Mom: Then what would happen? Would it heal?

Sami: Yes.

Mom: (KEY QUESTION) So if you fall and hit your head, you won't die. You might break something, but it would heal. Can you live with that, if the worst thing happens?

Sami: Yes.

Mom: How likely is it that you will break something?

Sami: Not very.

Mom: Then do you want to try it?

Sami: Sure.

I have found this exercise to be very helpful with children and adults. The nice thing about asking questions is that you don't have to have the logic, and it's a great way to uncover the fear. Once a fear is recognized and out in the open, it's so much easier to deal with. It really takes the sting out of it. (The same is true for secrets, but that's another story.)

Subconscious Fear

The final category of fear that I've experienced is subconscious fear. This is a fear that you may not even realize you have. I find this fear to be the most insidious because I don't recognize it very easily.

Subconscious fear shows itself most often for me in procrastination. I keep meaning to do that task, but end up finding 3,000 other things that seem more important. It takes a lot of self-discipline to sit down and do what I have to do. If I am really on my game, then I can ask myself, what is going on? Why are you struggling to finish this? It's often because of fear. Fear of rejection, fear of humiliation, fear of the unknown, fear of loss of control.

Writing this book has been the epitome of subconscious fear—not even fear, complete panic at times. Often, it has felt like I was riding on a very scary roller coaster without Dramamine—completely nauseating. I actually ended up back in therapy to deal with this because I hadn't experienced this level of self-doubt in years, if ever. Here's what I learned about this underlying fear.

When we have these unexplainable feelings of panic, fear, or doubt, our brain may be trying to tell us something. When we simply take every thought captive and weigh it against truth, then ignore it; we could be telling our brain that it's crazy and there's nothing to worry about. However, the limbic part of your brain is responsible for fight or flight, and it is trying to tell you that you have a large cause for concern and you should be prepared. When I ignored it or tried to rationalize it, my limbic brain got more scared and kept getting louder and louder until sometimes I was nearly paralyzed with fear. This is very disturbing when you are writing a book titled *Be Freaking Awesome.* My fabulous therapist said, stop trying to ignore it. Sit with it, and write down all the crazy thoughts in your head. Eventually you'll get to the actual fear. In my case it was fear of being vulnerable and rejected. Next, she instructed that I begin to make a plan for when I felt exposed or felt rejected (also weird because I often explain that rejection doesn't exist except in our minds). Was I going to call a friend and talk through what happened with my husband? What was my back-up plan for if the worst thing happened? By acknowledging the fear and coming up with a plan in the event of "disaster," I was able to reassure my brain that this was going to be okay, and it was safe to move to the next step.

I wish I could tell you that this was a one-and-done attempt, but multiple times I've had to take a few days to have my irrational freak out, then get back on the horse, so to speak. This is one of those times I have to explore the lie, "I have to have my crap together before I can write a book."

Fear of Failure

Fear of failure could be classified in all three categories of fear: subconscious, fear based on experience, and irrational. I would consider it subconscious because often I don't know that it's the fear I'm battling. It's based on experience, because if you've failed you know what that feels like. It's irrational because there's rarely logic attached to being afraid to fail.

Fear of failure is what holds many people from living their dreams. This is a common fear and one that I would have readily admitted to experiencing for most of my life. Above all else I didn't want to prove the voices in my head right. They said things like, "You'll never amount to anything." "You'll be lucky if you aren't addicted to drugs by the time you graduate high school." Etc., etc., etc.

I would say the best defense against fear of failure involves several steps. First, remember the Chinese proverb that says, "Fall down seven times, get up eight times." Second, study really successful people. They have failed in huge and epic ways. Sometimes very publicly. It's becoming pretty popular to fail big. Last, follow John Maxwell's advice and fail fast. Try new things, and figure out what works and what doesn't as fast as possible. Learn the lean start-up technique of pivoting. That means that when you discover something not working, have the courage to turn to the left or the right and find the best path for you.

I wish the answer to fear of failure was just go for it—whatever it is. It's rarely that simple. I would say you also have to assess where you are from a confidence standpoint. Meaning how willing are you to take risks? Think about doing something with little risk; how does that make you feel? Let's say you are going out to lunch with friends, and they ask where you would like to go. Saying what you really want to eat is a small risk. Are you comfortable with this risk? If not, then gradually expand your willingness to take on risk.

> *Fall down seven times, get up eight times.*
> *- Chinese Proverb*

Fear of Success

Recently it has come to my attention that I'm not afraid of failure. Instead I've become aware of a more bizarre fear, at least in my opinion. I have discovered that I am afraid of success. I'm afraid that if I'm really successful I won't be who I am anymore. I am afraid I will spend money in stupid ways, that I will forget my plans to help others when I am more successful. I am afraid I won't have friends because I will become snotty and mean. I am afraid if I don't have to trust God I will drift and wander. I have struggled most of my life to succeed; if I don't struggle, then who will I be?

How does all this relate to being afraid of success? I'm not entirely sure. I feel like I'm on a cliff preparing to go hang gliding, and I feel like I need to spend more time getting ready to get ready. Have you ever felt that way? What I know is that sometimes you have to step into the next part, and the path will be illuminated. Maybe only a few steps at a time.

To combat this fear of success, I reached out to my tribe. I called a few close friends and had this conversation: "Hey, if I get really successful and turn into a bonehead that forgets how to be a good person, will you smack me upside the head and remind me who I am?" It's a little disconcerting the speed that my friends agreed to kick me in the pants if I got "too big for my britches." It was also very reassuring to know that people would remind me who I am if I forget.

Fear of Rejection

What does it look like? Mostly it looks like playing safe. Why should we ask for what we really want when we might be rejected?

Jack Canfield says there's no such thing as rejection. If I ask you out for dinner and you say no, I didn't have someone to go to dinner with before, I don't have someone to go to dinner with after, and my life didn't change. In business, if we ask someone to do business with us and they say no, my business didn't change.

What changes is the emotional response we add to Canfield's equation. As we previously discussed: Event + Response (responsibility) = Outcome. We add negative thoughts to the event, such as no one wants me, no one likes me, I'll never find a date for dinner. These negative thoughts are what cause the feeling of rejection. Remember in the last chapter when I said our thoughts can cause our emotions? Here's a great example. What if we said, "Better luck next time," or "I'm sure they are busy and that's why they didn't go to dinner with me." When it comes to business, I've learned that my service is not a fit for everyone, so I consider it a blessing when someone doesn't choose me. I trust that the right clients are waiting just behind this person saying no. I also assume that if they say no they might have been difficult to work with, and I imagine that I've dodged a bullet. If all that fails, then I remind myself that the only way to develop perseverance is to experience setbacks.

Faith

Faith is being sure of what we hope for and certain of what we do not see. It's complete trust or confidence in someone or something. It is a great antidote for fear.

For me, faith is believing the best about whatever is happening. It is believing that eventually, even if things aren't going the way I want them to today, good will come from this situation. I think sometimes our faith is born from actual experience. Just as we can create fear based on actual experience, faith can be the same way. We can remember the times when things seemed to be really bad, but in the end, it worked out for the best.

The most obvious example to me occurred in the year 2005. I had been working with Barry on our software business since 2001. I was down to one client, and I was on-site consulting with them twenty-four hours per week. In my job I met with different departments to discover what they needed and identify pain points so we could solve them. I had a lot of hurt built up because for four years I had been the one in front of the client when the software didn't work. In the spring of 2005, after several days in a row of fighting about how something should be done—we were in our home and I was screaming and cursing about the software—I said, enough. I put in my notice with the client and told Barry that I wasn't going to work for the company anymore.

I felt it was time. I felt peace that things would work out and that God would honor my decision to prioritize my marriage before my job. I wish I could say that I felt a strong leading that this was what I should do, but really, I don't know that I was that tuned in. A year later I would feel differently.

In September, my Uncle Jim had a relapse from his lung cancer and died several weeks later.

A few weeks after the funeral, Josh jammed his finger for the second time in six weeks, this time needing surgery.

Barry's sister-in-law died of cancer in December.

His mom had a heart attack in January, which led the doctors to discover lung and bone cancer. She died about seven days after being told she had 6 months to live.

In the middle of that, we had bought a house to flip, but Barry was grieving too much to really help me with the flip house.

In late March, Lexi had her fourth case of strep throat in about three months. She was referred to an ENT and scheduled to have her tonsils and adenoids removed.

By May, I looked up and said, "oh my goodness." Since I'd decided to leave the business a year before we'd had two parents die and two of our kids had surgery. If I hadn't left the business and was still trying to work, there's no way I could have done it. This was another time I learned that obedience really is bliss. I know myself well enough to know that if I hadn't followed and obeyed, I would have been crying, "Lord, you said you wouldn't give us more than we can handle, and this is more than I can do." And it would have been my fault for not listening in the first place.

During this year, I didn't set a single goal; I didn't review a single character trait. I got up each day and took it one day at a time. The huge success was in the getting up every day. I know I grew that year, it just wasn't self-directed growth. I grew in my ability to listen to the still small voice in my head that told me enough is enough. I walked away from the business even though I had no way to replace my half of the monthly income. If you happen to be reading this book during a dark season, let me give you hope that there is light at the end of the tunnel—and usually it's not a train.

Faith is knowing all things work together for good for those who love the Lord. I don't pretend to understand all the pain and suffering in the world, I simply rest assured that God is sovereign. I believe God is in charge and we are not, faith gives us the ability to let go of fear and simply trust.

When I dare to be powerful - to use my strength in the service of my vision, then it becomes less and less important whether I am afraid.
- Audre Lorde

Some people drift through their entire life. They do it one day at a time, one week at a time, one month at a time. It happens so gradually they are unaware of how their lives are slipping away until it's too late.
- Mary Kay Ash

Life's problems wouldn't be called "hurdles" if there wasn't a way to get over them.
- Author Unknown

The difference between average people and achieving people is their perception of and response to failure.
- John C. Maxwell

It is not the critic who counts; not the man who points out how the strong man stumbles, or where the doer of deeds could have done them better. The credit belongs to the man who is actually in the arena, whose face is marred by dust and sweat and blood; who strives valiantly; who errs, who comes short again and again, because there is no effort without error and shortcoming; but who does actually strive to do the deeds; who knows great enthusiasms, the great devotions; who spends himself in a worthy cause; who at the best knows in the end the triumph of high achievement, and who at the worst, if he fails, at least fails while daring greatly, so that his place shall never be with those cold and timid souls who neither know victory nor defeat.

- Theodore Roosevelt

Set Goals

People with goals succeed because they know where they're going - Earl Nightingale

I joined Mary Kay Cosmetics when I was twenty-two. When I decided to earn my company car, I hung a poster of the red Pontiac Grand Am next to my bed. Every night I would fall asleep imagining what my car party would be like. When you earn a car in Mary Kay, your friends show up at the dealership to celebrate with you when you pick up the car—that's a car party. I would think about who would be there. I would imagine what it would be like to sit in the car (I had test drove the car at a local dealership to ensure my visualization was correct). Then I would say to myself every night, "Smell that new car smell." I would literally imagine that smell. Just twelve months after joining the company, I earned the car.

So, when I tell you to vividly imagine your ideal life, what are you going to do? Imagine your life, for goodness sake. Look back at the chapter on creating a vision for a level 10 life. Keep this vision in mind as you now set goals to get there. If you have a hard time with this part, consider a time in your life when an area was more like the ideal. What worked during that time of your life? Or think of a friend who seems to live ideally in a particular area. What do you like about your friend's life? Imagine yourself in it. I have total faith in you to do this.

Write It Down

In his book *Leaders Eat Last*, Simon Sinek explains how the four brain chemicals are used in motivation. Dopamine is the chemical that gives you a boost when you complete tasks. By writing down exactly what you want, you begin to use the natural way your brain works to get more things done. How many times have you decided to write down your to-do list after you'd already started working on a project, and you wrote down things you'd already accomplished so you could mark them off your list? That's because checking them off your list gives you a hit of dopamine, and your brain likes it a lot.

You've probably read the statistics that written goals are five times more likely to be accomplished. My favorite study had always been the one that followed graduates of Yale. The premise of the study was that they followed the class of 1953, and those who wrote down goals were twenty-five percent more successful. However, while researching the exact citation for this book, I discovered that it was an urban legend. Dr. Gail Matthews was disturbed by the urban legend when she read about it in *Fast Company*. She went ahead and conducted a study proving that the study may not have happened, but the premise is correct. "Research conducted by Matthews shows that people who wrote down their goals, shared this information with a friend, and sent weekly updates to that friend were on average 33% more successful in accomplishing their stated goals than those who merely formulated goals."

GRAND Goals

I have always loved goal setting. However, over the span of fifteen years, I began to notice more and more reluctance to set concrete goals. I didn't like to give them a time frame, and I stopped sharing my goals with others. I had created negative thought patterns, and my self-esteem eroded with each missed goal. Does this resonate with you?

A few years ago, one of my coaches, Kim Hodous, author of *Show Up, Be Bold, Play Big.* introduced me to GRAND goals.

GRAND goals are:

Guaranteed—What you think about you bring about. The Law of Attraction really does work.

Recorded—Writing your goals guarantees that you will at least remember them, and therefore you are more likely to succeed.

Authentic—Goals must be your own and true to yourself. Setting a goal because your spouse, boss, or parents want you to is a recipe for a failed goal.

Noble—Your goal must not be harmful to others. It must be good for mankind.

Daring—Goals should push you out of your comfort zone and cause you a little trepidation.

The idea is that you set GRAND goals in nine different areas of your life. I added a tenth, contribution/giving. We may decide to give of our time, talent, or treasure, but I believe when we give back to the world as an act of gratitude, our life is fuller and more complete. The 10 areas which correspond to the Wheel of Life are:

1. Family and friends
2. Personal growth and development
3. Spirituality
4. Wealth and finances
5. Business and career
6. Love and romance
7. Health and body
8. Play and fun
9. Contribution/giving
10. Artistic and creative (physical environment)

For me setting goals in these ten areas has created a situation that allows me to feel successful on a regular basis. Instead of working for days, weeks, months, or even a year or more to feel I've accomplished a goal, I can feel success daily. One of my family and friends goals is to have more girlfriend time. That means that anytime I get to hang out with a friend, I have accomplished my goal. A health and body goal is to eat less sugar. One night I went to a business after hours, and instead of eating a brownie, I only had fruit. I cheered for myself all the way home.

Take a moment to look at each area and think of at least one thing you could do on a regular basis that would begin to create a feeling of success if you accomplished it. You can also add more concrete long-term goals in the area to work toward. Give yourself time to complete the exercise over the next week so that you have at least three goals in each area.

After selecting at least three goals in an area, once a year you select three overall GRAND goals to focus on for the year.

Besides feeling success on a regular basis, it sets up a scenario to give you something to strive toward. Following Kim's advice, I aspire to rewrite my goals every seven days. This leads to feeling successful because I can see what I'm accomplishing. If I begin struggling to feel successful, it's typically when I've stopped this habit.

So far, we've assessed our life, defined what level 10 living is, identified character traits that we want to develop, and set GRAND goals in a number of areas. Officially you are ten years down the road from where I was from that nervous breakdown, maybe farther. When I read a book, I like to read all the way through before I go through and do the exercises. However, this book won't be nearly as effective if you haven't done the things I just listed. Take a moment and a piece of paper to write GRAND goals in each of these areas.

SMART Goals

Many of you may be accustomed to SMART goals. It stands for:

Specific | **M**easurable | **A**ttainable | **R**ealistic | **T**imely

For years I was a fan of SMART goals. I loved affirming on or before December 31, I will weigh 165 pounds and be in ideal health. But here's what would happen. I had two ways of operating. I would accomplish the goal and then not set the next goal, so I would slide back down where I had been before the goal was set and had to redo that goal again at another point. Or I would set a "stretch" goal that I wasn't sure was possible, and I would work my butt off to get there. I would have the attitude of shoot for the moon and you'll still land among the stars. But over time, as I mentioned, it began to erode my self-confidence. I began to notice that as soon as I set the goal something would happen to give me an excuse not to have accomplished the goal. I would get sick, my kids would get sick, we would have a car accident, something.

This would further kill my self-confidence to the point that I would doubt myself about weird small stuff. Outwardly, I looked successful. My thought life was crap.

I stopped going after SMART goals, I thought I'd sworn them off for life. But I realized the GRAND goals weren't giving me the same drive and motivation. I knew there had to be a better way.

Combining SMART/GRAND

In the book *Switch: How to Change Things When Change Is Hard*, Chip and Dan Heath explain that we have two parts of our brain, the rational part and the emotional part. They use an analogy that the emotional part is like an elephant and the rational part is like the elephant's rider. The rider can help guide and direct, but the elephant is still a giant animal with a mind of its own. GRAND goals help me set the vision of what I want my life to look like in ten different areas. According to Chip and Dan, we have to create a vivid picture of where we are going and why it's worth it to engage the emotional side of your brain—the giant elephant.

SMART goals give me a way to measure my progress along the way. SMART goals engage the rational side of the brain— the rider. The rational side likes clear direction on where we are going. Once the rational side of your brain understands where you want to go, it will stop fighting you, and it will begin figuring out how to get you there.

Another concept shared by Chip and Dan for accomplishing change is finding bright spots. It's the classic advice: reward good behavior and ignore bad behavior. Catch them doing something right. We went through several parenting studies when our kids were little, and one of them said, in addition to praising good behavior, affirm the positive behavior trait the child was displaying when they did that behavior. "That was very kind of you to share with your brother." "Thank you for respecting your sister's wishes to not have her hair pulled."

Essentially, finding bright spots is like parenting yourself. By choosing each day to review my day and make a list of five successes of the day and match those to my GRAND goals, I am able to find the bright spot and keep moving toward the target of my ideal life.

GRAND goals give you vision; SMART goals help determine the path. Rational and emotional sides of your brain are high-functioning. Elephant and rider are working together.

What if I don't know where to start

If you are unsure of what your goals should be, perhaps it would help you to look at life as seasons instead of time on the calendar. Many people say to me, "I don't know how you have the time or the energy to do all that you do." They didn't know me in the preschool season. My children were five, two, and newborn when we first bought our business. I spent most of my time doing diapers, bottles, play dates, and early bedtimes. I have joked that for me, preschool was the longest prison sentence I served. I knew I had to pour into my children, I knew I wanted to be there for them, but it was exhausting. I think as stay-at-home moms we don't tell the story enough that it's really, really hard work. I can remember saying to my husband, "don't touch me; I have been pawed at all day long and I just need to be able to lie in bed without someone touching me."

Then the elementary years came, and they were in kindergarten, second grade, and sixth grade. I actually took a couple of years off work during this phase. I was really nervous that I would screw up the teenage years, so I wanted to take some time to re-center my parenting. I had no idea this was the calm before the chaos. Not emotionally, but the busyness of activities in junior high and high school was very intense, both in time and money. As they started band, competitive soccer, and other school-related activities, life became so busy. We tried to keep the number of activities to two or three, which works until junior high. This is the time they want to explore and see which activity or interest is going to stick. There was lots of car time, which is when I tried to hold to the rule that if kids were in the car I wouldn't talk on the phone because this was the most significant amount of time I spent with them. If you really tune in, they will talk to you. Well, the girls did. My son really talked in the car when it was just the two of us and he was driving. He couldn't be on his cell phone or radio, so he would talk more.

During these seasons—preschool, elementary, junior high—I had a lot less time that was exclusively mine to do what I wanted. As each one began driving, my time freed up a bit more. Then they started going to college, and now I have a lot of time that is completely at my discretion. In some ways, I miss the car time, but I've tried to be intentional with each season so I don't live with a lot of regrets. Obviously, there are times I could have been more attentive. I could have traveled a bit less or been less self-absorbed, but overall, I am pleased with my efforts. My goals during each season were very different. Prioritizing date night during the preschool years was critical. Now we have so much time when it's just the two of us, we aren't as fanatical about it.

As you set goals, be aware of what's going on in your life. You may not be able to go as fast as you want to go, but that doesn't mean you can't find time to carve out for yourself.

When I decided to finish this book in 2016, I had to set the alarm for 5:30 AM every morning because I figured out that after working all day, I wasn't very creative and I was less likely to actually sit down and write when I could hear my family hanging out after dinner. Don't use the season you are in as an excuse, make time for your goals.

Daily Check-in

When we are starting out with goal setting, our rational brain kicks in, and we believe we have to not only set the goal, but we also have to know how the goal will be accomplished. You may not know all the steps needed to accomplish your goal, but you probably know the key things you can do to move yourself in the right direction. In The Power of Consistency, Weldon says that when we begin to visualize our ideal life, we can think about the one or two things that we know would move the needle. Each goal has one or two items that, if you did them consistently every day, you would get much closer. It is helpful to write this down so you can be clear on what you will do, so when you do it you can celebrate and be excited about your progress.

If we are clear on what we want and then we focus on those one or two things, our minds and the Law of Attraction will begin to work on our behalf.

For instance, this year we decided to get healthy. I have affirmed in my GRAND goals for four years that I wanted to weigh 165 pounds in a healthy way. I stopped there and never figured out what one or two things I could do to make a difference Finally, I decided to dramatically reduce my dependence on carbs—I love bread and pasta—and prioritize protein. Last year, I started the year at 192 and by the end of the year had finally lost 19 pounds. Not all the way to my ideal weight of 165, but much closer.

In addition to affirming things that work, Chip and Dan Heath discuss a concept to script critical moves. As much as we'd like to believe we have full self-control all the time, we don't. If we can decide in advance what we will do in critical situations, it will be easier to make good decisions and stay on course. For instance, I love hamburgers. I have scripted the critical move by deciding that when I eat a hamburger I can cut carbs by eating it on a lettuce wrap.

Share with Safe People

Part of your plan to accomplish your goals must involve sharing them with at least one other person. I used to say that you should tell everyone you know about your goals so they can hold you accountable. However, what I've learned is that some people just aren't very safe with your dreams. I've learned that hurt people, hurt people. Also, your plans or goals may change, and if you have told everyone you know, they may not get it when you pivot and change direction. So, find safe people in your life so you can share your goals—people who can encourage you even if they don't understand. In the beginning, this may just be one or two people. Hopefully it can include your immediate family members. It often doesn't include parents. Parents are designed to protect you, and often that need to protect you conflicts with their desire to encourage you. If your parents are different, and I pray they are, that's fantastic, because parents can be your biggest and best cheerleaders. If your parents aren't supportive of big dreams, don't let it bog you down. I don't have parents anymore and have just found other people to fill those roles. My friend, Dick says if he could adopt a forty-year-old woman, he would do it. He and his wife are fantastically supportive of my hopes and dreams, as well as being very intense when critiquing my speeches to help me improve.

Review Daily

In addition to telling someone, you have to review your plans daily. That means that you need to either post a reminder on your bathroom mirror, beside your bed, or perhaps on your computer monitor. The best thing is to review your goals each morning and rewrite them once a week. In his book *The Power of Broke*, Shark Tank's Daymond John discusses how he has goals he writes in his notebook, and he reviews them at least five times per week. If it's good enough for Daymond, it's good enough for me.

More important than a clean house
is a close family.
- Ann Voskamp

If you're not making mistakes, then you're
not doing anything. I'm positive that a doer
makes mistakes.
- John Wooden

Begin to Be Freaking Awesome

A year from now you may wish you had started today. - Karen Lamb

A day comes when you have to wake up and decide: today I'm going to start. If you didn't do that this morning when you woke up, you can start in the middle of the day. But you must start. You must say, I'm good enough, I'm smart enough, and doggone it, people like me. Okay, you don't actually have to mimic Stuart Smalley from Saturday Night Live. What does it look like? Before you go to bed, go to the mirror, look yourself in the eye, and say five times, "I'm enough." (Have you been doing that homework?)

Next, review the day and make a list of three to five things that went well. Choose to forgive yourself or others and not dwell on the things that didn't go well. Next, review your goals. After your goals, consider the one or two things you need to accomplish to complete your goals. Do you need to get up early? If so, set your alarm accordingly. Read a book or devotional that supports one of your goals. Finally, fall asleep visualizing your ideal life. - how you want it to be, as we talked about in Chapter 2. Finally, sleeping after learning is essential to help save and cement that new information into the architecture of the brain, meaning that you're less likely to forget it.

When you roll out of bed in the morning, review your goals. If possible, read them out loud. Once a week, rewrite them. Review the character traits you want to have so they will be fresh on your mind. Next, go to the mirror, look yourself in the eye, and say five times, "I'm enough" (yes, twice a day). If your spouse thinks that's weird (ask them to read the book), you can do it in the car at stoplights. Review the list of one or two things you need to do to move the needle on your goals. Plan your day so that you get those one or two things done.

Then as you go through your day, consciously raise your self-awareness. If one of the character traits you are working on is being kind, then when you go to work, be kind. It doesn't matter if people think you are weird. As long as you haven't set the goal to be a horrible human, people around you will get used to your newfound desire to be kind.

Enjoy the Journey

Think about the last time you went on a vacation. Did it go completely smoothly? Were your flights delayed or did you get lost? Did the glitches ruin your trip, or did it create a different memory and more stories? Rarely do trips go 100 percent as planned. Often these glitches create a situation that adds to the story. One time I was flying to Las Vegas to do training for a client. My flight was rerouted because of a storm in Denver, so I landed in Phoenix, stayed on the plane with some passengers while others departed. By the time we left for Las Vegas, we were at least three hours later than expected. But we were flying to Vegas, so no one was in that bad of a mood. Silly and slap-happy tired, but in good spirits. The flight attendant was beginning to bring drinks. I mentioned that it's really irritating when you order a Coke at a restaurant, and they say, "Is Pepsi okay?" We talked about how that is not the same and it's super annoying. For some reason, this brought up the fact that I liked Dr. Pepper and sometimes they substitute it for Mr. Pibb, which is actually a good substitute. So, when the flight attendant asked me what I wanted to drink, I said, "Mr. Pibb." She said, "Oh sorry, all we have is Dr. Pepper." About thirty people in the back of the plane started laughing, and we couldn't stop. We were crying we were laughing so hard because we'd stop laughing then look at one another and start laughing again. It was silly—the flight attendant looked like she was going to start random drug testing—but it made the flight much more tolerable. We all chatted the rest of the flight and started our time in Las Vegas on a happy note instead of grumpy that we were delayed for three hours.

How do you handle setbacks? What do you do when you find yourself falling into the old patterns of not living the character traits you want? Do you get grumpy, throw up your hands, and say, this is never going to work? Or do you figure out a way to pick yourself back up, laugh a little, and realize this is part of the journey? I would encourage the laugh-a-little response. Sometimes we say, someday this is going to be really funny. Might as well be today. Why wait to find joy in the midst of struggle?

Rhythms of Life

If you spend much time with me at all, you will know that I often say, "Everything is better when you can see a palm tree." That being said, I don't live in a beach setting. I live in Northwest Arkansas where there are four distinct seasons, and the trees go from beautiful buds and blossoms to rich leafy green to beautiful autumn colors. One of the things we did when the children were small is to "drive down the mountain" from Fayetteville to Alma to see the leaves when they change color. Based on my very driven personality that loves adventure, this seems sort of a pedestrian way to spend a Saturday. But I just love the changing of the trees.

When I'm not in beautiful Northwest Arkansas, I love to go where the palm trees grow. Florida, Hawaii, California, or the Caribbean are places that just restore my soul. I think because typically to have palm trees you must have water or ocean. The gentle sway of the ocean waves allows all my cares to drift away.

On a trip to St. Kitts, I walked along the beach. On some parts of the beach, my feet sank in deeply. I had to move slowly and carefully, but I still made progress. This reminded me of life's obstacles that slow down our journey. They can be loss, a need for healing, or just flat out disappointment. They are just part of life.

During another part of my trip across the beach, my feet didn't sink in hardly at all, and I left very few impressions. I was able to move quickly and easily. This reminds me of when my journey has been smooth and relatively easy. Fortunately, there are times in life when things just click. It seems that everything I touch turns out well. Relationships are at peace, I easily rectify wrongs I've done, and all is right with the world.

I also observed that at times my feet sinking in the sand left impressions of average depth, not too deep, not too shallow. To me this represents the most common part of our journey. Our life is made up of a whole lot of days that aren't on the beach. It's work, laundry, dinner, kids' activities, the normal rhythms of life. This is the stuff that makes life become so mundane and routine. During this time, it's important to find the spice. It could be a walk at lunch, noticing the spring blooms, or really appreciating your family. Something enjoyable that helps break up the monotony of life.

On your journey, know that life isn't all about the peaks and the valleys, there's a whole lot of monotony. I tell my kids, be sure you like the person you marry. Most of the time you don't spend being husband and wife, a whole lot of time is spent on life logistics, and when you do life with your best friend, it's a whole lot more fun to endure the monotony.

It's a Choice

When people ask me how I'm doing, I've developed a new habit of saying, "I'm fantastic." I guess after this book, I'll have to say, "I'm freaking awesome." And no matter what, I really am. The more I say it the more I feel it. How is it that I'm fantastic? I think of the places I've been and the people I've known.

Chennai, India, 2001—the streets were filled with filth. When we walked down the street with a wrapper left from our sandwich, we looked and looked for a trash can. Our host assured us that we could just throw it on the ground. Imagine the trash everywhere you looked as a result of this attitude. The average teacher there made 820 rupees a month – approximately $16. That is what I would spend taking my three children out for fast food. The smells were completely overwhelming. The pollution from cars, the constant aroma of curry, the smells were non-stop and very intense.

The people of India were incredibly hospitable. They knew we couldn't drink the water, so each evening after our activities, they had an assortment of bottled soft drinks and cookies. They were warm, welcoming, and wanted to make us feel as comfortable as possible. My absolute favorite was hearing their stories. The joy they had despite their lack of material comfort or possessions was humbling and inspiring. When I think of all my blessings and all the things that we take for granted here, I am fantastic. I have clean air, clean water, a bed, and a roof.

Identity

When we are still wounded, we look for our identity in all sorts of ways. Since I was bounced around so much as a kid, I tried really hard to be perfect so people would allow me to stay. Since ultimately, I continued to move to the next family, I began to believe a lie: that no matter how hard I try it's never good enough. This wreaked havoc on my career, my parenting, and my marriage. This lie I believed was so insidious that it still whispers in my head.

There are whole books dedicated to identity issues. I want to simply cover the fact that you need to think about where you get your identity. Brené Brown says that no matter how much you get done or not, if your task list is complete or not, you are still enough. Whoa, the first time I read this, I was pretty far along in my journey, and it still made me take a step back. If I couldn't measure my worth by what I did, what I accomplished, how much money I had, then what in the world was I supposed to use as a measuring stick?

What do you mean I'm not supposed to use a measuring stick? I am enough, just as I am. Just because I am breathing. What? This is a very hard concept to grasp and walk upright in. So much of my life has been mired down in shame. Even after I began the process of healing, I still had so many lies I believed that deeply affected my day-to-day life.

If I was enough just as I am, then I don't need my husband's approval for business decisions. I don't need someone's approval for what I should wear. I have thought, "I wonder if this is what the CEO of a marketing agency is supposed to wear." Then I followed it up with, "I guess it is, since you are a CEO and this is what you are wearing."

Here's the thing about being enough, just as you are. You then become a whole lot better at creating space for other people to be enough. If I don't need my children to be perfect for me to be okay, then they can just be who they are.

In 2013 I went to work for one of my clients as Vice President of Sales and Marketing. I thought I was doing a great job because I thought the owner wanted me to run the business like I owned it. Near the end of my time with the company (their choice, not mine) I had to take a deep look at what I valued. Where I was getting my value. Just before I lost my job, I had asked for prayer for my carpal tunnel that was acting up. I mentioned that I felt like I had to learn to walk again. Mainly because I had to begin to learn not to get my identity from my job. One day my boss was really upset, which meant I was really upset. I went to the bank at lunch time. I was completely stressed out. I remember standing in the teller line, and I finally had the sense to whisper to God, "Lord, how do you want me to think about this situation?" The calmest sweetest thought crossed my mind, which I believe was God speaking to me, "You don't get your worth from that job or that man. I have this, do not worry, do not fret, be strong and courageous and calm."

I instantly calmed down.

The situation didn't change. However, my perspective changed, which allowed me to think more clearly and more creatively. It also gave me peace when I lost my job a few weeks later and had to figure out what to do next.

Thinking differently didn't stop me from losing my job. However, with my new perspective of "enough-ness," I was better able to imagine my next role or returning to my own company and what it would be like if I were to succeed at it.

In his book, *Start: Punch Fear in the Face, Escape Average and Do Work that Matters,* Jon Acuff says, "You don't need to go back in time to be awesome; you just have to start right now. Regretting that you didn't start earlier is a great distraction from moving on your dream today, and the reality is that today is earlier than tomorrow."

Today, this moment, begin to Be Freaking Awesome.

It always seems impossible until it's done.
- Nelson Mandela

I had as many doubts as anyone else. Standing on the starting line, we're all cowards.
- Alberto Salazar

You must do the things you think you cannot do.
- Eleanor Roosevelt

Most good things have been said far too many times and just need to be lived.
- Shane Claiborne

Forgiveness says you are given another chance to make a new beginning.
- Desmond Tutu

Imagination is the beginning of creation. You imagine what you desire, you will what you imagine and at last you create what you will.
- George Bernard Shaw

Peace begins with a smile.
- Mother Teresa

Every great dream begins with a dreamer. Always remember, you have within you the strength, the patience, and the passion to reach for the stars to change the world.
- Harriet Tubman

Course Correction

*The majority of men meet with failure because
of their lack of persistence in creating new plans
to take the place of those which fail.*
- Napoleon Hill

There are going to be times when you stumble and fall down. How long it takes you to get back up is just part of the story. I started writing this book in 2014. I got eighty percent done with the title *Lessons from the Sailboat*. When I was in my late twenties, I said to my mentor, "I'm tired of struggling. I feel like I'm constantly rowing my boat upstream." She said, "Then stop." I thought that was stupid and proved that even the person who knew all my darkest secrets didn't really know me. I was driven, I was going somewhere, I was not going to let life knock me down. During this time, God said to me, "Sweetheart, the reason it seems like you are rowing upstream is that you are on a sailboat and you are trying to use oars to row the boat and that's not how it works. I need you to go up to the deck and stand behind the wheel. I created you to steer the boat; we will decide together which way we will point the sails. But know this: I am the wind. You will not be able to go anywhere without me filling your sails." This is a beautiful metaphor that shaped a lot of how I've lived my life—at least when I was living consciously and not on autopilot. So, I thought I should name my book *Lessons from the Sailboat*.

I took a sailing lesson in San Francisco, I sailed in Portland during World Domination Summit. However, I found that I couldn't imagine giving that talk over and over again for five years. As a professional speaker, you often give the same talk tweaked to the audience for relevancy. I just couldn't get excited about that talk. So, at eighty percent complete, I just stopped and said, "Lord, let me know when it's time to finish."

It took two years. While giving a talk to a direct sales group on vision, motivation, and taking care of their people, I said, "You guys, here's the bottom line: Just be freaking awesome. That's it." One of my friends in the audience wrote in huge letters in her journal, Be Freaking Awesome by Angela Belford. Then she wanted a picture with me and that note and casually said, "Someday this will be us taking a picture with the cover of your book." It was like a lightning rod. I knew that it was the title of my book. I suddenly had more motivation than I'd ever had.

When you stumble, fall down, and don't immediately pick yourself back up, please be kind to yourself. It's still part of the journey. I mean you get through a road trip faster by not stopping, but if you have to stop awhile, just be sure to start back again...eventually.

Take a Deep Breath before Reacting

In his book *Triggers*, Marshall Goldsmith talks about things that happen to us that trigger emotions that we may not understand. How many times have you reacted in anger to what you thought someone said and then figured out that they didn't even say what you thought they said, much less mean what you thought they meant? Maybe for the rest of your life, but for sure while you are in this season of learning to *Be Freaking Awesome*, when someone says something that triggers a negative emotion, stop. Take a deep breath. Next, tell them what you thought you heard them say. Ask them to confirm. If it still triggers a negative feeling, see if there's a gentle way to get out of the situation or delay the conversation a bit. If you have a supportive person communicating with you, you may say, "Hey, I'm not sure why, but for some reason that caused me to feel really upset. Would you be willing to let me talk about why?" If the person is insecure or unfamiliar with such processing, it may not go well. I have tried to say this to Barry, and often it made him defensive about what he said. After many arguments that didn't go well, I had to say, "This is not about you. Why does everything have to be about you? Why can't I sometimes unravel the crazy in my head?" Not productive or kind, but I finally got through to him. We talked about the drawbridge and not raising the drawbridge, but now we need to talk about what caused you to want to lift the drawbridge to begin with.

This part can be time consuming, and there are different schools of thought. Some say you don't need to do a lot of digging to find the root cause of the beliefs that cause the feelings. I like the path of least resistance. That means if I can just identify a behavior, decide it isn't serving me, and stop doing it, I'm all for it. The question is, when you are tired, stressed, hungry, or sick, are you able to stop doing this behavior? In your worst condition, will you be able to stand by your decision to be more kind or to not get angry? Not to say you won't have a bad day, just that if your new behavior requires a great deal of self-control, then when you are weak the behavior won't stick.

I find that if I can find the root cause, discover the lie I've believed or the false belief, change it to a positive belief, then when I'm tired, stressed, or hungry, the behavior actually is in alignment with where I want to go. For instance, because of spending a lot of my childhood being food insecure (not knowing where each meal was coming from), as an adult with children I would have a panic attack if we ran out of milk. I usually tried to mask the panic by yelling at my husband for some dumb thing that he may or may not have done. It didn't matter if I had the money to shop and had just ran out of time; I felt like a complete failure that I couldn't keep food on the table. When I finally realized I was upset about not having milk, I began to say different things to myself. "Okay, you don't have milk. You have a car, you have money, and the store is open. That means right now if you needed it you could go and get milk. Do you need milk right this minute? No, okay, when do you want to go get milk? Later today or tomorrow." By converting this to a problem that was just a math/time problem to be solved, I wouldn't spiral out of control. It took a while to figure out what the trigger was.

Lately, I have had a random thought when someone opens the small cabinet in my kitchen. I think "That is more food in one cabinet than in the whole house of many of the places I lived as a child." Now that my kids are older and I'm healthier, if they complain about us being out of some food they want, I say things like, "You have money that I give you, and you know the way to the grocery store as well as I do."

Triggers outside of your control

Memorial Day after eighth grade, my family went swimming at a local campground called Cove Creek. My stepdad and I were swimming when he said, "Do you think you can swim to the island in the middle?" I said, "I can if you can." So off we went to swim to the island in the middle of the cove. It didn't look too far away. I wouldn't say I was a great swimmer, just the arrogance of youth to do anything you set your mind to. Every now and again, I would let my legs drop to see if I could touch bottom. The longer we swam, the more tired I got and the more I started to freak out. I got to a point where I knew I didn't have the energy to let my legs drop and then kick them back up again to keep swimming. I swam a little longer but finally reached the point where I couldn't move anymore. I was convinced I was going to die for nothing at the very beginning of my life.

We were still about 100 yards or more from the shore. I don't really know how far it actually was. I only know that I gave up. I prepared to drown. It was the most awful feeling in the world. I stopped swimming and stood up in water that only came up to my chest. My stepdad immediately yelled at me for not telling him it was not too deep. Apparently, he only kept going because I was still swimming.

Despite many, many attempts to get over that day, I still cannot control the panic attack that often happens when I feel out of control in the water.

But I kept trying. I chaperoned Sami's 8th grade float trip. At the end, everyone would "ride the wave" by floating down with just your life jacket through the last rapids. I wanted to join the fun, but a face full of water and subsequent panic attack meant Sami at fourteen was grabbing my face saying, "You're OK, Mom. You're OK."

We went white-water rafting in North Carolina, and there was a section of the river where we could get out of the raft and float with our life jackets. I was doing great until the rapids started getting stronger. I was swimming as hard as I could through the panic attack and still couldn't reach the boat. Finally, the guide from another boat plucked me out of the river with such ease that I was able to calm my panic attack by the time I got back to our boat with my kids. But when I got back to the car, where I thought my kids couldn't see me, I completely lost it, ugly crying and all.

Still I wouldn't give up. I put it on my goal poster to stand up paddle board. A historically clumsy girl with a major panic issue in the water shouldn't haven't the goal to stand up paddle board. But I HATE having fear control me.

Barry and I were vacationing again in St. Kitts and decided that this was the perfect place to stand up paddle board. When we rented the paddle boards, we were warned that with twenty-two MPH winds we might not have an easy time. It had been so long since I'd been in the water that it didn't occur to me to put on a life jacket. Barry and I paddled out away from all the people swimming. My first attempt to stand was successful and easy, but I couldn't steer with all the wind. So I sat down to paddle to the location I wanted, away from the boats and the more choppy water. I am paddling along when I thought, "This is silly. What's the worst that can happen if you stand up? You'll fall, no big deal." So I stood up and was doing well until the water got a bit choppy and off I went. I was underwater for less than five seconds, but it felt like an eternity. I was very thankful that the rational part of my brain was loud enough and strong enough to say, "Just stay calm and keep swimming." But that part of my brain was fighting hard against the irrational part of my brain, screaming at me, "Why didn't you wear a life jacket? Why did you think this was a good idea? This was so stupid." My brain was flooded with panic and adrenaline. I had to swim about twenty feet to get to my board, which also felt like an eternity. I grabbed my board, climbed up on it, and completely lost it. I was crying while trying to look around and see Barry. I could see that my paddle was stuck in the floor of the ocean, which meant again I had panicked in water that wasn't very deep, less than seven feet. The after effects of a panic attack SUCK. No matter what you tell your brain, you have to let the emotion bleed off a bit. After twenty-three years, Barry has lived through more than his fair share of these water-induced attacks. He's so kind and gentle and strong when it happens. This time when it was over, I ended up crying on the shore for a really, really long time. I cried harder than I'd cried in years.

The next day on our trip we were hiking beside the Atlantic Ocean along the lava rocks when a wave that I didn't see knocked me into the ocean (in a riptide zone). My only thought was grab a rock to avoid being pulled so you aren't pushed out to sea. I stood up on a rock, but and the next wave pushed me onto the rocky shorelineknocked me further into shore. Typically, if the first wave didn't trigger a panic attack, the second one would have, for sure. This time, even though when I stood up, my leg was swollen and bleeding from my knee to my ankle and it looked as though . We both thought I'd broken my leg, I didn't feel the fear.

I had been seriously in danger, and I didn't panic.

I managed to limp back through the rocks back to the sand for the remainingstill half- mile hike back to the car. I was elated. I was trying to jump up and down. Barry thought I had hit my head because I was so excited.

This place of refusing to allow my fear to control me and living with the knowledge that for those few minutes, it does control me is what keeps me trying again and again. Maybe now this fear is put to rest, or maybe I'll still have to face it. At least now I know I've overcome it when I had to.

Green Hair

When thinking about triggers, it's important to introduce the Green Hair concept, taught by Jack Canfield. I think it resonates with me because when I was kid and when my kids were younger, by the end of the summer the daily exposure to chlorine caused our blond hair to actually be green. Assuming this isn't the case, imagine if someone walked up to you and said, "Hey, you have green hair." How would you respond? Would you be upset? Offended? No, because you know that you don't have green hair.

Let's say that I am secretly concerned that I'm not a good mom. Then someone makes a comment like, "Are you going to let your kids do that?" If I perceive they are questioning my ability to parent, then I may either get my feelings hurt or I may get really angry and say things like, "Who do you think you are to question my ability as a parent?" They may be completely caught off guard by this and not know how to respond. They may also defend themselves against this seem- ingly unnecessary attack and cause this to escalate.

If I am confident I'm a good mom, then when someone questions my ability to parent, I will consider the source, then decide if what they are saying has value and not be offended. I know I don't have green hair so when you say I do it won't matter

My son, Josh, was packing to go to college, and my husband was a bit teary-eyed (he's the sensitive one). He commented to my son that he couldn't help it. Then my son said, "That's okay; Mom won't even miss me." They both laughed. Then later in the car my son said this to me again. I didn't react at all. I looked at him and said, "Not my issue, so that doesn't upset me. You know I love you and want you to have awesome adventures, and then come home and tell me about them when you can." I wasn't offended, hurt, or even really amused, I knew he was trying to tease me, and it didn't get to me.

Later that day our dog was in the basement and wanted upstairs, and I had this random thought: "Josh won't be down there to be with our dog anymore" (his bedroom was in the basement). Then I started crying uncontrollably for at least thirty minutes. I needed to mourn the changing of the seasons in my own time and be okay with the process. I was glad I hadn't gotten offended earlier in the day so I didn't have anything to apologize for.

If the Green Hair doesn't resonate maybe my friend, Rick's version will. He says if you are playing catch with your kids and suddenly you pick up dog poop and throw it at them, will your kids catch it? No, they will move out of the way. The problem for us as adults is that people throw dog poop (say mean things, tell us we aren't good enough, etc.) at us and we think we are supposed to catch it and make it our own. It's their crap, just step out of the way and let it fly past you. Then you don't have to spend time dealing with the effects later.

Imagine the Situation Differently

You will come to situations where you aren't sure what to do. You will know what you usually do in that situation, but you won't know how to handle it in a healthy way. Here are a couple of things to remember. First, think about how someone with the character trait you are trying to emulate might do it. I wanted to be a good mom. My mentor, Paula, was a good mom. There were times I would say, "How would Paula handle this situation?" The ideas may not be how Paula would actually handle a situation, but by stopping to think, I allowed my mind a chance to come up with ideas instead of a knee-jerk reaction.

The second idea is to learn to trust yourself. During this process, I have encouraged you to be curious about everything. You may decide that you have reacted poorly in most situations in your life. You may decide that you can't trust yourself. Fight this feeling with all your worth. Add to the affirmation that you say in the mirror. In addition to "I am enough," say, "I am wise." Or "I am discerning." Or whatever resonates with you. Just don't believe the lie that you can't trust yourself. It's the worst feeling, and it doesn't serve you on this journey.

Success is about dedication. You may not be where you want to be or do what you want to do when you're on the journey. But you've got to be willing to have vision and foresight that leads you to an incredible end.
- Usher

Those who dare to fail miserably can achieve greatly.
- John F. Kennedy

When you start living the life of your dreams, there will always be obstacles, doubters, mistakes and setbacks along the way. But with hard work, perseverance and self-belief there is no limit to what you can achieve.
- Roy T. Bennett

For every failure, there's an alternative course of action. You just have to find it. When you come to a roadblock, take a detour.
- Mary Kay Ash

Before success comes in any man's life, he's sure to meet with much temporary defeat and, perhaps some failures. When defeat overtakes a man, the easiest and the most logical thing to do is to quit. That's what the most men do.
- Napoleon Hill

Only I can change my life.
No one can do it for me.
- Carol Burnett

Renew Your Commitment

Success consists of going from failure to failure without loss of enthusiasm. - Winston Churchill

We've talked about the fact that to change the cycle you've been living in you must first make a decision. That's true. Remember when I told you that to Be Freaking Awesome you have to wake up and start? The next day, you have to wake up and start again. The day after, you have to wake up and start again. It means deciding each day that you are going to Be Freaking Awesome. It's like taking a bath; you don't just take one and be done forever. You have to get clean on a regular basis.

In *Triggers* Marshall Goldsmith also says that his research has found that by asking yourself six active questions you can make better progress toward your goal. Writing down the answer to these and knowing you will ask them of yourself, helps you throughout the day to stay on course. He goes on to say that just asking the question, "Did I do my best?" instead of, "Did I accomplish...?" puts you in a course-correcting mindset.

Active questions:

Did I do my best to set clear goals today?

Did I do my best to make progress toward my goals today?

Did I do my best to find meaning today?

Did I do my best to be happy today?

Did I do my best to build positive relationships today?

Did I do my best to be fully engaged today?

These may not be your six questions, Marshall shares that he tweaks the last few based on what goals he is currently working on. Consider defining your questions to help you toward your goal.

Accountability

As you look at where you want to go and the roadblocks you have to remove, you may find you are not able to go on this journey alone. You may need some therapy or coaching or simply an accountability partner.

Therapy helps people look at how things that happened in the past are affecting behavior in the present. Coaching typically looks at where you want to be in the future and helps you attain that goal in manageable steps. An accountability partner is someone else on a similar journey who you can reach out to when you are weak. They are there to remind you what YOUR goals are and you remind them of their goals so you both stay on track.

When I was a Mary Kay consultant, I called these people running buddies. I had a friend in another unit who was also working toward earning a car. During this time of intense qualification, you have an opportunity to experience a lot of nos. Which can really get you down. My friend Cathy and I would call each other nearly daily to talk about what our plan was for the day and how many calls we needed to make or appointments we needed to book. We would then check in after we got our stuff done to affirm that we had been successful. I had a similar opportunity with my upline, but it was easier to be whiny with my upline. If I didn't do what I told Cathy I said I was going to do, I was embarrassed. It was way more effective. During different seasons of the business, I had different people provide this accountability, and I recip-rocated. On days when I experienced an insane number of nos, Cathy would remind me that another day I had gotten an insane number of yeses. When we are down in the valley, it's sometimes hard to remember what we learned in the sunlight on the mountain top. A good running buddy can be the reminder.

Caution, you have to choose someone as committed to the goal as you are. Spouses typically make lousy accountability partners. When you are having a rough day, you don't want your spouse to try to hold you accountable. You want encouragement, understanding, and reminders of your goals. At least in my experience, I don't need a kick in the pants from my husband. So, consider having an accountability partner not related to you or married to you.

I think the advantage of having someone who is on roughly the same path is that empathy is much higher and the path seems less lonely. I've been accountability for people when I was much further down the road than they were, and occasionally they expressed that they felt all alone in their challenge. I had been through it, but they didn't get to reciprocate and remind me when I was down, making it less effective. It was more coaching than accountability.

When you first begin the journey, two things may happen. First, you may have great success with identifying issues, removing negative beliefs, and really making progress. This is exciting and fun. It will motivate you to keep going. Or, you may not have much success removing negative beliefs and making progress. You may find that you do well in self-awareness—you finally realize that you are hurting people and making them upset—but you don't really know what to do to stop it. A good accountability partner can help shine a light on the path at your feet. This may be the time you need a coach who can really give you the kick in the pants you need.

A few years ago, we met with a financial advisor and set our financial goals. I told him how much I wanted to have saved by the end of the next quarter. Then I set up my appointment with him the next quarter. I know myself; when I'm tired I don't want to dig around the kitchen to find something to eat. I want to grab something on the way home. When I was tempted to eat out, I would think of telling our financial advisor that I hadn't met my realistic goals and would feel silly. Then, I'd go home and make myself dinner.

Many of us get tired, stressed, or sick. When we are at our worst, it's the most difficult to stay on track. By asking someone else to hold you accountable, you are forced to share the junk in your head with another human. When you are tempted to falter, you can either call the person holding you accountable or you can imagine having the conversation where you tell them you faltered and why. Often this potential embarrassment is enough to keep us on the straight and narrow.

Therapy

I would be remiss if I got through this book without sharing my philosophy on therapy. If you were raised by humans, you will probably need it at some point. If you were raised by wolves, you may not, but with human parents it's almost a sure thing.

Here's why. We are all doing the best we can with the information we have right now. If you could do better, you would. When you learn better, you will do better. That means that while your parents were raising you, they were doing the best they could, but they had their own hang-ups, fears, and issues.

My kids used to storm off mad at me, and sometimes I would say, "I'm going to write down what I actually said and what actually happened, so when you are talking to your therapist they will have my side of this story and not just the twisted-up crap in your head right now." My oldest would say,

"Mom, you probably shouldn't affirm that we will need therapy." The truth is, we are all humans, and we twist some crap in our heads sometimes. Before I went to therapy the first time, I believed that if I were a good mom, Sami would be a good child. So, if she wasn't good, that was a reflection on me not being a good mom. That means, I encouraged perfectionism at a high level. It's nauseating to me now to see how I needed her to dress well, act well, and be perfect so I could be okay. When she was a teenager struggling with perfectionism, I would say, "Sami, your mom has been to therapy and is okay; you don't have to be perfect to prove she's okay. You can just be yourself." She would tell me how weird it was for me to talk about myself in the third person. I've tried to help coach her through her perfectionism, but at some point, she may need help unraveling the crap in her head.

Sometimes the first therapist you see won't be a good fit. That doesn't mean that therapy isn't for you, it just means that therapist wasn't for you. The therapist I saw during this time when I needed Sami to be perfect was horrible. He said to me, "She's two, what do you expect?" He never connected my need for her to be perfect with me not being okay. I went to three or four visits and gave up. Two years later I found Joe, and it stuck.

Mentor

In addition to accountability and therapy, you may also consider a mentor. A mentor is someone who is farther on the path than you are, and you can just observe what they do. Everyone thinks they need to have it all figured out before they can be a mentor. I believe you just have to be a few steps ahead of where the mentee is. Sometimes it's helpful if they are way ahead, but sometimes that makes them less relevant if it's been too long since they experienced what you are going through.

Paula was my mom mentor. Her youngest was a year older than Sami, and her oldest was about nine years older than Sami. I guarantee I've made way fewer mistakes in my parenting because I had her as a guide. I've watched how she handled all sorts of situations. I also got to ask questions about how she felt about different choices her kids were making. It made it okay for me to feel what I was feeling because I didn't feel so alone.

When looking for a mentor, I recommend you be clear on what you are looking for. Start by inviting someone to coffee a few times. See if you connect and can be real with the person, and find out if she is able to be real with you. Then perhaps ask if she will meet you quarterly for coffee to bounce ideas off of them. Consider ways that you can add value to the relationship. You want to be interested in this person's life because that's how you can observe how she handles different situations.

Also, think about who you could mentor. Who is behind you on the path that you can help along? How can you be intentional about sharing the lessons you've learned? In today's world of four generations in the workplace at the same time, you may find situations that can be a reverse mentoring. Consider how an older colleague can teach a younger person how to navigate politically charged situations, and then a younger person can help teach the older colleague about new technology that is cool, new, and relevant.

Be a teacher to all below you,
Be a fellow traveler to all on the same level,
Be a student of all above you.
- Jack Canfield

Celebrate Success

Celebrate your successes. Find some humor in your failures. - Sam Walton

As you go through your day, you will have the opportunity to accomplish goals. One of my GRAND goals is more girl-friend time. Any time I get a chance to have a long chat with one of my friends I get excited to recognize I'm accomplishing my goal. Several years ago, my coach, Kim, assigned me the task of finding a physical touch point when I've accomplished a goal or made the right decision. It could be a fist pump, it could be the fist pulled toward the body with arm bent (often seen by NFL quarterbacks), whatever gave me energy. I chose to mimic Molly Shannon's Superstar pose from Saturday Night Live. Sometimes I'm not in a situation where I can do the pose full throttle, but even saying Superstar! gives me a mini burst of joy.

As you begin to Be Freaking Awesome, find a physical touch point that is going to give you that victory sensation for accomplishing even a vision goal. If your goal is to make healthier food choices, then when you order salad instead of pasta—celebrate.

In her book *Presence*, social psychologist Amy Cuddy discusses a study of blind children who participated in the Special Olympics. Upon crossing the finish line, they threw up their arms in a V sign, threw back their head, and pushed out their chest. They never saw anyone else do this: they just instinctively knew this is what victory felt like. It was a natural expression of celebrating success.

We also need to celebrate our success with freedom. When we become adults, we begin to develop ideas that we have to act mature, that we must act our age and be respectable. I'm not advocating ruining your reputation at work or with a client by becoming obnoxious, but you have an inner child that still lives inside you, and she gets extremely impatient if you are going to be a stick in the mud all the time. Find a time and place that you can adequately celebrate your success. What feels like physical celebration to you? Is it jumping up and down? Is it doing a happy dance? Is it screaming at the top of your lungs, beating on your chest? You may have to experiment a bit with what really gets your blood pumping.

After you find the over-the-top, maxed-out version of celebration, you also have to find a version that can be done while sitting at your desk at work, in your kitchen, or wherever you experience successes. Perhaps at your desk you can sit still from the waist up and dance your feet. Or maybe it is a full chair dance. In the kitchen, it could be throwing your arms up in the air. You have to celebrate when you have success. Your body has to know this is what it feels like to accomplish a goal. You could be celebrating a goal such as, I will call and check on my mom once a week, or it can be that you chose fruit instead of a brownie. The key is to get your body in a state of accomplishing goals a lot so that you can begin to really trust yourself, and when you set a goal you know it's going to happen.

Write It Down

We write down the goals we are going to accomplish. I believe it's just as important to write down the goals you have accomplished. You can put this in your gratitude journal, you can start a new place just to track goals, or you can make a poster. I personally don't write it on my goal poster on a daily basis because my goal poster is pretty abstract. The longer I've done goal posters the more I've put concepts that represent a way of life rather than specific things to do or places to visit. At the end of the year, I jot notes on the back of my goal poster to remind myself of how the things on the poster came true.

One coach suggested I keep a file folder of successes in my desk, and if I was having a rough day or had a rough phone call, I could refer to that file of successes and increase my energy again.

Find what works for you, but you have to write it down. When things are going poorly, the only things you can remember are the things that went poorly last time. When things are going well, we sometimes are tempted to slack off and forget what got us to this point of success. By keeping a success log, you can refer to this to keep you on track.

Rewards

All work and no play makes Angela a very dull girl. We set GRAND goals, we set SMART goals, we write down our success, we do a little physical celebration. If that's it, over time your inner child will decide that you can't be trusted with her best interest in mind. She wants to have fun and a lot of it. You have to program in rewards for yourself. There are certain goals that would be so much more satisfying if you could plan a reward. Here's where I've tripped myself up sometimes. Let's say that I have a weight loss goal. To celebrate, I don't want to reward myself by going out to eat. If I have a goal to pay off a lot of debt, I can't go into more debt by taking a reward vacation.

You have to include the resources necessary to reward yourself as part of the goal or pick something that doesn't involve those resources. Think of the things you like to do that you often don't feel you have time or money to do. It could be visiting a cool museum, perhaps you collect things and your reward for a big goal is to add to your collection, or maybe it's going to the movies with friends. Plan a party to celebrate. Notice that many of the things on this list involve experiences or people. For me, that's how I celebrate. Maybe you like to read lightweight romance or playing video games. Perhaps if you get your work done for the day, you give yourself permission to read twenty minutes of guilt-free fiction. Whatever it is, you have to figure out how you will reward yourself when you accomplish big and small goals.

Coming together is a beginning;
keeping together is progress;
working together is success.
- Henry Ford

Great minds discuss ideas; average minds
discuss events; small minds discuss people.
- Eleanor Roosevelt

Reaching Your Destination

What you get by achieving your goals is not as important as what you become by achieving your goals. - Zig Ziglar

At some point, you'll encounter a situation that makes you realize you've accomplished one of your character traits. Perhaps your spouse makes an unreasonable statement, and instead of getting angry you simply ask for clarification, state what you heard, get more information, and have a civil conversation about why you disagree. Then you may notice that something a bit different triggers you. Get curious about why, plan your next journey, and begin the process again.

At some point, you will review your goal list, and you will notice that you have begun to accomplish some of the GRAND and SMART goals you have set. Since you're already in the habit of celebrating those successes daily and weekly, it's important to recognize how far you've come. Take a few moments to review where you were when you started the journey, all the roadblocks you worked through, and the character traits you now see in yourself. It's important to spend time in this step of the process, because the next time you encounter something hard that you have to grow through you will be able to look back on this time and remember that you do have what it takes to work through this new challenge.

Life Is a Journey

While on vacation or soon after I arrive home, I begin planning my next vacation. Some people think this signifies a lack of gratefulness. But for me, it represents that life is not stagnate. I believe you are green and growing or dead and dying. There is no staying the same. Can I be more loving today than I was yesterday? Can I be more kind today than I was yesterday? Can I be more productive today than I was yesterday? Then Be Freaking Awesome today!

As you set goals and then accomplish goals, remember how we talked about considering the season of your life plays into those goals. If you are single, it may be necessary to set goals that involve spending time with others and scheduling family time or not working too much. If you are in the midst of preschool or elementary years with your family, you may need to prioritize finding alone time to read, write, or do personal development. Whatever season you're in, don't fall into the comparison trap: If only I were married, I would be able to XYZ. If only my kids were older, then I'd be able to ABC. Whatever it is, appreciate your situation, your season, and set goals that support the kind of life you want to live.

I often say one of my top measures of success is that as my children become adults they like me and trust me, as well as being ready to be productive adults. Perhaps you already have a tumultuous relationship and don't have that trust and enjoyable relationship. Figure out what you can do to improve yourself to make that relationship make sense. Maybe it's nothing. Sometimes kids choose their journey. But do you use every encounter as a way to share love or do you share your disappointment? Think about it, and set the goal to be better today than you were yesterday at showing love to your child.

Don't Get Stuck on a Plateau

Sometimes we have worked really hard to get to a new level of excellence and character strength. It is tempting to think we've arrived and we are here to stay. It is a balancing act to celebrate our success and not feel like we've earned the right to "rest" and stop working on our stuff. As I've mentioned, we are either green and growing or dead and dying. There is no holding pattern that we can be in for very long. If we decide to rest, that means we put our guard down and we might begin to slip back into old patterns. We've had those old patterns for a really long time; the grooves in our brain are deep. These new patterns haven't yet had time to become habit. It's like making a new path through the woods. If it isn't continually walked on, the weeds are going to grow up, and you'll have to redo the work. Better to stay on your game continually. Inertia is a beautiful thing. It says that a body in motion stays in motion. If you can stay intentional and self-aware, it's easier than losing focus and then starting again.

Think about weight-loss diets: Many are crazy extremes that no one can maintain. There is definitely value in shocking your body out of its comfort zone—I have had to do this with my carb addiction. But quickly I realized that I needed to find a way of eating that I could maintain for the rest of my life. This seems counter to taking it one day at a time, but that's because this is a different season. When you are first starting out, you do have to take it one day at a time. After you've developed your goal-achieving muscles, you need to find a way of living that is sustainable.

Set the Next Goal

So how do you set the next goal? Go back to your list of character traits that you aspire to develop. If you've been working on perseverance, then perhaps now you want to be more spontaneous. Choose your next character trait that you want to develop. When it comes to positive character traits, you will spend the rest of your life becoming more of the person God created you to be. Remember, you are either green and growing or dead and dying; there is no such thing as stagnation.

In addition to character traits, when you set your GRAND goals, you selected the top three that were the focus. This can be done annually or this can be done as you accomplish the goals and need to reset. I have had a few goals that took several years to attain. Usually, it took some time because it was tied to a financial goal or it took a while to save up the money to accomplish the goal. One of my goals was to redo the floors in our main living area and kitchen. This involved not only saving the money, but also researching the best option for flooring to cover both areas. Then we moved on to actually doing the demo work and putting down the flooring. Once we started, the whole project took two weeks—each evening tearing something up, moving furniture, and putting down the flooring. Because of some other goals, it took about a year and a half to get to that two weeks.

We Are Goal-setting Machines

Back in August 2002, I set the goal to pay off $20,000 in debt by March 1, 2003. When we paid off the debt, we were going to buy a new house and hire our first employee. We were living in 1,300 square feet with three children under nine. We had converted our garage into an office, and my mother-in-law spent about four to five months with us each year. I made a list of all the things I wanted in our next house, and my husband made a list of what he wanted in the next house.

I was focused and determined. Weird things happened to keep us on track to meeting this goal. Our car was in a hail storm and was totaled by the insurance company, but it was completely drivable. We landed contracts we'd worked on for years. We got to December, and we had paid off $10,000. My husband said, "Are you going to set a new goal?" I looked at him confused. He said, "We've paid off $10,000 in five months, we can't do $10,000 in two months." I told him that I would change my goal on March 2 and not a day before.

I subsequently met a potential client and had a meeting on February 10. He said he would buy our software with two conditions: 1. With training, taxes everything, it has to come in under the $10,000 state bid limit; it doesn't make sense to bid it if your price is $10,500. 2. You have to install it and train on it before March 1.

With software, we get paid at installation. I left the office shaking with excitement. I called Barry, and he said, "I just got off the phone with a girl from our small group at church, and she has a friend who just graduated and is looking for a job in programming." I then told him about the contract.

A few days later I was bringing Sami home from a school dance, and I decided not to take the turn to go to our house. She asked where we were going, and I said, "I don't know. I just feel like I'm supposed to drive this way." A short bit down the road, I saw a real estate sign. It was a deserted area of the road, so I stopped, backed up in the road, and then turned down the street. I did this a few more times until Sami, then in third grade, said, "Mom, if you don't know where you are going, you may want to slow down." I never did listen to that advice. I finally pulled up to a house that had a sign that said "price reduced, pool." I pulled out the flier, and it was like reading our list of what we wanted in a house. That weekend there was an open house. When we talked to the Realtor, he said, "It's been on the market since August, but I've never had an open house until this weekend. We walked through the house and decided it was more than we could have dreamed. The walk-out basement with separate bathroom was perfect for our business office.

We started prepping our house for sale and put it on the market just as an ice storm hit Fayetteville. The same day I was to do training. Fortunately, I was able to get to the training, and by the time I called Barry at my first break, we already had six people interested in the house. Within six days of listing the house, we had a full-price offer with no contingencies, and we were approved for a mortgage on our dream house.

Great story—I love telling it.

Here's the cautionary tale. I didn't set another goal after meeting the house goal. I thought I'd arrived; I thought I was just going to coast and live the dream. When I looked up two years later, I was completely miserable in my job. I wasn't making any progress toward saving; I was just coasting. I didn't have another goal. Sure, I went to work painting the house and doing some work to make it ours, but I didn't make a decision about the kind of person I wanted to be, the kind of marriage I wanted to have, and the kind of business I wanted to develop. So, it stayed about the same, except I'd gotten a whole lot less happy about my job.

In his book, *The Happiness of Pursuit,* Chris Guillibeau talks about what it was like to set the goal to visit ten countries, then expanding the goal to visit twenty countries and then finally he expanded it to every country in the world. It took him ten years to complete the quest. Can you imagine chasing the same goal for ten years?? Imagine the costs, the time and the experiences. After he completed it, he, of course, wrote a book about what he learned. He also decided to interview many other people that had completed epic quests to see if there was universal things to learn. My favorite thing that he shares is that once you've accomplished a goal, you'll never be the same. No one can take away the experience, the education or who you become.

After you've accomplished a big goal, you might review and ask yourself these questions:

What do I need to keep doing?

What do I need to stop doing?

What do I need to start doing?

You have to set another goal—no coasting allowed. If you don't, you may even slide back down the hill you've just climbed up.

It's harder to stay on top than it is to make the climb. Continue to seek new goals.
- Pat Summitt

I can't change the direction of the wind, but I can adjust my sails to always reach my destination.
- Jimmy Dean

Never doubt that a small group of thoughtful, committed citizens can change the world; indeed, it's the only thing that ever has.
- Margaret Mead

Gratitude can transform common days into thanksgivings, turn routine jobs into joy, and change ordinary opportunities into blessings.
- William Arthur Ward

Vision without action is merely a dream. Action without vision just passes the time. Vision with action can change the world.
- Joel A. Barker

To improve is to change;
to be perfect is to change often.
- Winston Churchill

Music can change the world because it can
change people.
- Bono

The whole point of being alive is to evolve into
the complete person you were intended to be.
- Oprah Winfrey

Winners never quit and quitters never win.
- Vince Lombardi

If we are always arriving and departing, it is
also true that we are eternally anchored. One's
destination is never a place but rather a new way
of looking at things.
- Henry Miller

I always liked those moments of epiphany,
when you have the next destination.
- Brad Pitt

It's not the destination that matters. It's the
change of scene.
- Brian Eno

Share What You've Learned

No one lives long enough to learn everything they need to learn starting from scratch. To be successful, we absolutely, positively have to find people who have already paid the price to learn the things that we need to learn to achieve our goals. - Brian Tracy

When we are going through something hard, it isn't always easy to see what lessons we are learning. Often it is after we get through the hard time that we realize what we learned. I believe that telling the story helps us to recognize the lesson we learned or perhaps the lesson we need to learn. Perhaps in the process of sharing your story, you'll realize that you did develop the character trait you were looking for and you hadn't realized it yet. There are things I know, and there are things that I know well enough to teach. I assure you, every time I teach I learn something new. I also learn the material at a new level. When we are willing to share with others what we've learned in a way that allows them to learn from our mistakes, we learn the lesson at a deeper level.

I meet people all the time who are surprised by the hard things I endured as a child. From age ten to twenty-five, I never told my story. I wanted to forget all the bad stuff that happened to me. I wanted to pretend that I was normal. It was a secret that made it very hard for me to be close to anyone. I had a fear of abandonment because of all the people who had left me, and I was in a self-fulfilling prophecy loop because I would push people away before they could abandon me. The strange thing is that pushing people away meant I still was alone. I didn't see that for a long time.

After the third round of therapy, I slowly started telling parts of my story. What I found is that lots of people could relate to different things that happened to me. Then instead of people seeing me as this driven, type-A person who didn't have a heart, they began to see that I did care a lot about people. I was probably a lot like hugging a porcupine. If you could get past the prickly parts, I was pretty soft on the underside.

The other thing that happened is that sharing my story made it safe for others to be more open. This was especially true in church settings. People believe they have to put on a good face so they will be accepted in church. And in some churches, that's probably true. But I tried to make it okay to not be perfect, to not have a perfect childhood, to make bad choices as a result of that childhood, and still trust God in the end.

I believe that shame festers and grows when we live in secrecy and hiding. In hiding, we believe that if they just knew everything we had done, they would never like or respect us. They would stop being our friends. Typically, I have found that if someone believes this it's because of insecurity and maybe unresolved perfectionism.

Remind Yourself of How Far You've Come

Another reason to share our story is to recognize how far we've come. Sometimes we are going along setting goals, accomplishing goals, growing in small increments. With the passing years, you discover a character issue you want to work on, and you may say, dang it, I thought I'd resolved this. Healing is like an onion. You peel away a layer, and you may go along just fine for a while. Then something will trigger you that will cause you to realize there's another layer that can take the healing deeper. Since it's been a while since you peeled away the last layer (or last four layers), you may not recognize how much you've grown since the beginning of your journey.

When I was frustrated and feeling like I was still stuck in the same place, my friend, Sweetie said, "Have you thought about going to see Joe?" I hadn't thought of Joe in a long time. It had been twelve years since I had last received counseling from him. She encouraged me to go back to him for a few visits to review the progress I'd made in that time. At the same time, I was taking a life writing class, designed to teach you how to write your memoir. Joe asked me to share the writing with him from the class. These two experiences were transformational in my perception of my journey. I came to see that things that had once been significant triggers, things I thought I'd never get over, were no longer even an issue for me. I realized how much forgiveness work I had already done. This is also the period when I recognized that while I forgave the original act that hurt me, each time I had a consequence from the hurt to deal with I had to forgive the person for the transgression again. It's like if someone cuts off your foot, and you forgive them. Then every time you fall down because you don't have a foot and you get mad again, you have to forgive them for the way your life will be different forever. Maybe eventually you won't get mad, but until then forgive again.

By telling my story to Joe and taking the life writing class, I appreciated just how far I'd come.

A Point of Connection

Many times, when we have things happen to us and we don't share our story, we begin to believe we are the only one this ever happened to. When we share our story, we have an opportunity to connect with others who have a similar story. I know someone who experienced a sexual assault and ongoing sexual harassment while in the military. When she reported it, the incident was covered up and she was told for years that this had been her imagination. She recently connected with Wounded Warriors Project and during a retreat she shared her story. One of her fellow participants approached her to share that she had experienced nearly the same thing. While it didn't change her circumstances, she finally had someone who understood what she had lived with for all these years. It didn't instantly heal her, but it validated her feelings and gave her a friend to support her in her journey of healing.

It's scary to be real and it's okay to be cautious when you first start. We all know people who overshare too early in a conversation or relationship. Being freaking awesome includes being authentic about your story and what you've learned.

If you do not tell the truth about yourself you cannot tell it about other people.
- Virginia Woolf

You CAN have it all.
You just can't have it all at once.
- Oprah Winfrey

A word of encouragement from a teacher to a child can change a life.
A word of encouragement from a spouse can save a marriage.
A word of encouragement from a leader can inspire a person to reach her potential.
- John C. Maxwell

Give Others Grace

Empathy is the starting point for creating a community and taking action. It's the impetus for creating change. - Max Carver

There's a funny thing about being on the journey to health—you notice other people's unhealthiness a whole lot more. At first this sounds judgmental: You are unhealthy and I'm healthy. That's not the point. I'm saying that when you were a mess you needed a lot of grace. You needed people to overlook the overreacting when you were upset; you needed them to be kind when you were unkind—again. So as part of giving back, I want to encourage you to give grace. Grace is undeserved favor; it means we didn't earn what we are given. Our world needs a whole lot more grace, love, and peace. If you can be part of the solution instead of part of the problem, then please do. It doesn't typically cost us to give grace. Often, it's easier than getting upset and being mean when others are mean. Being mean, angry, and all the other negative emotions take a lot more energy. They also are not good for your health. So, for your sake and the sake of world peace, give more grace.

Love Yourself

When you want to spread more love, begin with yourself. The greatest command is to love your neighbor as yourself. What I see so often is people loathing themselves; I wonder how they could possibly love their neighbor when they can't stand themselves. What does self-love and self-care look like? For starters, it is being true and authentic to your whole self. The child that lives inside you gets really mad when you never have fun. The adult in you gets really mad when you don't follow through on your promises, such as saving money. You have to consider your whole self and find ways to nurture that part of you.

Whether it's creating fun situations, listening to great comedians, or watching movies, you have to take care of you. I love watching movies in the theater. I think it comes from when I lived with my aunt and uncle in Ohio. We didn't go to the movies very often with three children. But when Aunt Mary would take my two cousins with her to visit her dad, I would stay home with Uncle Jim, and often we would go watch a movie on Saturday night, typically something with Burt Reynolds. Not sure how Aunt Mary timed her every-other-year trip with a Burt Reynolds movie release, but there you have it. It was such a treat to go out with him. Also, as I got older, the movies were a place I could get completely caught up in the story and forget about my life for a few hours.

I also love to live a very full life. I typically run my life full throttle, and I love to travel. It's so interesting to meet new people, have new experiences, and have complete down time. I especially love going to the islands where my cell phone doesn't work, and I can really unplug. I get extremely fussy if I haven't been on a good vacation in at least a year. But I know some people hate leaving home. I recently heard someone say that they hadn't been on an actual vacation in seven years. If it's energizing to you and it feeds you, then do it. Figure out what feeds your soul. Do not compare yourself to others. I used to feel bad that I liked to travel so much. Not anymore. I just accept that it's a part of my personality and spend money accordingly.

Love Others

When you love yourself, you are able to love others well. You come in contact with your family, friends, coworkers, the weird guy at Walmart, and a variety of other people. Every encounter you have is an opportunity for you to love others.

According to author Gary Chapman, there are five languages of love. He starts his book, *The Five Love Languages* with a powerful story of imagining yourself in Russia, admiring the buildings in Red Square. All around you people are talking and it's obvious to you that the people around you are also admiring the buildings, but you don't know what they are saying because they are speaking in Russian. However, if suddenly someone says in English, "Wow, look at those colors," you instantly hear them even if they are many feet away from you. The more clearly we can learn to speak the five languages the better we can communicate the love we feel for others.

The five languages are Words of Encouragement, Acts of Service, Gifts, Physical Touch, and Quality Time. My number one love language is Words of Encouragement. That means that the easiest way to show me you love me is to tell me how awesome you think I am. The way to hurt my feelings the easiest is to tell me how much I've disappointed you. As you look around at the people in your life, how can you show them you love them, in a language that they can hear?

Now that you're farther down the road to Be Freaking Awesome, you're celebrating success and reaching your destination. You have what others need. It's time to give back.

Mercy is not giving someone what they deserve.
Grace is giving someone what they don't deserve.
- Andrew Wommack

Courage is grace under pressure.
- Ernest Hemingway

Grace is sufficient even though we huff and puff
with all our might to try and find something or
someone that it cannot cover. Grace is enough.
- Brennan Manning

Grace is God as heart surgeon, cracking open
your chest, removing your heart - poisoned as
it is with pride and pain -
and replacing it with his own.
- Max Lucado

Love each other or die.
- Mitch Albom

Love grounds you. It orients you. Love brings
your awareness to others and yourself. Love
opens your mind and heart to others and
yourself. Love settles you and gives you balance.
- Gary Zukav

You've gotta dance like there's nobody watching,
Love like you'll never be hurt,
Sing like there's nobody listening,
And live like it's heaven on earth.
- William W. Purkey

Inspire Others

The people who are crazy enough to think they
can change the world are the ones who do.
- Steve Jobs

As you go through life, you will encounter others who are considering taking the journey to health. Sometimes the beginning feels like the scene from an Indiana Jones movie when he comes to a giant gorge and there seems to be no way across. His dad cries out in his mind to Indy, and suddenly he gets the idea to take a step. It's a huge step of faith because if he's wrong he's going to fall to his death. As you cross many gorges on the journey to success, you can do your part to make the world a better place by encouraging others who need to take that first giant step even though it looks like it will land them in the bottomless gorge.

Encouraging others could include sharing this book, telling your story, posting positive uplifting posts to Facebook, or just being a bit nicer. It could be sharing the lessons you've learned as you chat with friends at coffee or reaching out when you see someone struggling. Whatever it looks like for you, somewhere along the line you gained the courage to start the journey. If you see someone else needing the courage, do your part to nurture that courage and remind them that they can do it.

Be Authentic

You can inspire others by being truly and completely authentic. I know there are varying degrees of authenticity. But what would happen if you decided to stop faking it? What if you decided to be your whole self, every day? What if you take the risk to live a wholehearted life? Do you want to experience more joy? More peace? More love? It begins with authenticity.

When we are authentic, we get to take off the mask; we decide to be okay with the warts and imperfections. When we do that, we make it okay for others to begin to let down their guard. Then we can breathe and feel like the work that we've done on the journey of success is finally worth it.

Be Open

As you go through the journey, be open to opportunities to pour into another. Some call it mentoring; some call it paying it forward. I call it necessary. There are so many young people raised by humans who aren't willing to do the work required to be a well-adjusted, healthy parent. When this happens, high school and college students are left wondering if the way they were raised is only way to do things.

I can't tell you how often I tell college kids, "Just because that's how you were raised doesn't make it right." Maybe you need something more formal than waiting to bump into someone who needs a mentor. If so, consider Big Brothers Big Sisters, volunteering with your church's youth group, Girl or Boy Scouts, volunteering to coach a sport, becoming a friendship family for an international student—whatever it is, your life will be enriched when you are open to giving back.

Where I am

I started writing this book in 2014. I spent that year surprised I was still married. The previous year I had decided that Barry wasn't interested in growing, so I was going to ask for a divorce. However, he reached a point that he didn't like himself anymore and decided to pursue health. The first few months, I totally didn't believe that he really wanted to work on himself. I wouldn't listen to his stories from working with his counselor. I told him, "You've said this stuff before and been able to stick with it for three months at a time, so talk to me in four months. After four months, I said, "Thank you for getting healthy for me finally." He laughed and replied, "I didn't do it for you. I did it for me. That's why it worked."

That first year of his journey was really bumpy. We had created some really bad communication and relationship habits and essentially had to learn how to be in a healthy marriage. I had to spend more time healing and not constantly reminding him of all the things he'd said and done over the years. It took a lot of effort, and we did it poorly more often than not. However, I'm happy to report that although we are still on a journey we are stronger than I ever imagined possible. We enjoy connection and intimacy that I thought was only in fairy tales and self-help books.

In my hometown of Fayetteville, most people only know me as a business owner and public speaker. I have shared my story in one-on-one situations for years, but not in this public way. Last fall I began a new policy that when I was asked to speak at a conference I only did Be Freaking Awesome. I have been surprised at how widely it resonated with such a diverse group of people. I thought it would be primarily for the direct sales industry, but it has become a leadership development training that spans the age and educational gamut.

It has also inspired a new chapter in my volunteer career. In the fall of 2016, a friend was telling me that he believed that with a proper strategic plan we could eliminate homelessness in Northwest Arkansas. I told him I wanted to help. I didn't want to serve on some dumb committee that didn't do anything, I didn't want to plan an event since I'd done that for twenty-five years, but if my skills and talents could be used, I was in. After a week of thought, he suggested I consider being the Community Ambassador for 7hills Homeless Center, where he served on the board. After a few weeks of research, I decided I would be the Community Ambassador for homelessness and lead the effort to create a strategic plan to eliminate homelessness in our community. I joined the board of the Northwest Arkansas Continuum of Care, the group officially tasked with creating the strategic plan. This board is required to have a person on the board that has experienced or is currently experiencing homelessness. That is me, and I often say this is the face of homelessness, thirty years later. Within four months of joining, I was elected board chair and had taken a team to Washington, DC, to be trained by a national strategic planning consultant.

Writing this book has brought up many insecurities I didn't know were still lying dormant. I've had to face my massive fear of rejection and failure and my even greater fear of success. I have found that the most effective way for me to keep going is to speak on the subject because when I see what an impact it has on people's lives and the ability to change their life even by one degree, it makes it worthwhile to continue to pursue the healing needed to bring this work to the world. Some days eliminating homelessness seems easier than overcoming the self-doubt and my fears.

I hope you will join me on this lifelong journey to Be Freaking Awesome.

Please visit my website (www.AngelaBelford.com) and join my email list. If you loved the book, tell everyone (especially Amazon reviews). If you didn't love the book, you can fill out the contact form on my website and when I'm having a good day, I'll read it.

Special thanks

I'm so richly blessed with dear friends. Among them I want to give a shout out to Robin, who originally taught me what unconditional love was as my college roommate and partner in crime. Your heart is beyond measure and my life wouldn't be the same without your unending love and support.

I also have saved literally thousands of dollars in therapy by the rich blessing of my friend Viki. You cry with me, laugh with me, challenge me to be my best, walk through the darkest days and love me well. It is your friendship that created the name of our publishing company, CBC Global - as in Crazy Blond Chicks.

I have to thank Attila Berry for being my final editor. Before you, I didn't really like my book. Thanks for making it better. Also, my beloved team at The Belford Group that deal with my OCD self very well and helped make the layout and design beautiful and amazing.

This book would be 1000 pages if I listed everyone that loved and encouraged me to finish this book. Your support means the world to me.

REFERENCES

Obviously, I love to read and here are the books I quoted or recommend. I keep meaning to publish my reading list. It could happen some day.

Acuff, Jon. *Punch Fear in the Face*. Brentowood, TN: Lampo Press, 2013

Allen, James. *As a Man Thinketh*. Mineola, NY: Dover Publications, Inc, 2007.

Brown, Brené. *Rising Strong*. New York, NY: Random House, 2017.

Brown, Brené. *Daring Greatly*. New York, NY: Gotham Books (member of Penguin Group), 2012.

Canfield, Jack. *The Success Principles*. New York, NY: HarperCollins, 2005.

Chapman, Gary. *The Five Love Languages*. Chicago, IL : Northfield Publishing, 2014.

Cuddy, Amy. *Presence*. New York, NY: Little, Brown & Company, 2014

Duhigg, Charles. *The Power of Habit*. New York, NY: Random House, 2012

Ferriss, Timothy. *The 4-hour Workweek*. New York, NY: Harmony Books, 2009

Frankl, Viktor. *Man's Search for Meaning*. Boston, MA: Beacon Press, 1946

Godin, Seth. *Leap First*. Louisville, Colorado: Sounds True, 2014

Goldsmith, Marshall and Mark Reiter. *Triggers*. New York, NY: Random House, 2015

Guillebeau, Chris. *The Happiness of Pursuit*. London, UK: Pan Macmillan, 2014

Hartmann, Thom. *Attention Deficit Disorder: A Different Perception*. Grass Valley, CA: Underwood Books, 1993

Heath, Chip and Dan. Switch: *How to Change Things When Change Is Hard*. Toronto, Canada: Random House Canada, 2012.

Hodous, Kimberly. *Show Up, Be Bold, Play Big*. Fayetteville, AR: Kim Hodous, 2012

Hill, Napoleon. *Think and Grow Rich*. New York, NY: Gildan Media Corp, 1937.

John, Daymond and Daniel Paisner. *The Power of Broke*. New York, NY: Crown Publishing Group, 2016

Long, Weldon. *The Power of Consistency*. Hoboken, NJ: John Wiley & Sons, 2013.

Katie, Byron. *Loving What Is*. New York, NY: Harmony Books, 2002.

Ryce, Michael. *Why Is This Happening to Me... Again?! : And What You Can Do About It!*. Theodosia, MO: Michael Ryce, 1997.

Sincero, Jen. *You Are A Badass: How To Stop Doubting Your Greatness*. Philadelphia, PA: Running Press, 2013.

Sinek, Simon. *Leaders Eat Last*. London, UK: Portfolio, 2017

Sinek, Simon. *Start with Why*. New York, NY: Penguin Group, 2009